AF593889

THE LITTLE BOOK OF ASTROLOGY

THE LITTLE BOOK OF ASTROLOGY

Fabienne Tanti

Mois de l'Immaculée Conception.

CONTENTS

MARS.
AVRIL.
I
II
LE BELIER.
LE TAUREAU.
Le soleil entre dans ce signe vers le 20 Mars.
Fable: Phryxus, fils du roi de Béotie, sacrifie au dieu Mars la toison d'or du bélier qui l'avait sauvé.
Les signes du Zodiaque.
Le soleil entre dans ce signe vers le 20 Avril.
Fable: Jupiter prit la forme d'un taureau pour enlever Europe, fille du roi de Phénicie.
Voir au verso

ASTROLOGY, A WAY OF LIFE

From the very moment we humans are born, we are interconnected with the cosmos. As soon as this interdependence is established, we are given the opportunity to develop our potential and give meaning to our lives while retaining our free will. In this regard, astrology studies the relationship between celestial motions and terrestrial events. It can therefore be considered a branch of metaphysics. It encourages us to look at ourselves, others and our environment. It also enables us to analyse and better understand ourselves, and to evolve. It is a key that opens the door to self-knowledge. By allowing us to advance, it also becomes a philosophy and a way of life!

Individual and universal knowledge

Astrology teaches us not to judge and is interested in the individual. It goes against today's trends, where appearing and having are more important than 'being'. By taking an interest in astrology, we look at ourselves in a mirror to better understand the reason for our experiences and existence, which also shapes our future. Mundane astrology, on the other hand, is concerned with our collective destiny and worldly events. It allows us to understand the evolution of countries based on the planetary periods of the slowest-moving planets and on the angles, known as aspects, formed between them.

The long history of astrology

Over the centuries, people have endeavoured to portray astrology as a superstition, overlooking the fact that it had long been a recognized science and discipline. Indeed, astrology has existed since the dawn of time. Prehistoric peoples were already observing the sky and knew that each thing had its specific place in the universe. The first written record of astrology appears to date back 4,000 years to the Mesopotamian civilization, with the discovery of the first astronomical compendium, the *Mul Apin*, in Nineveh, Iraq. Engraved on stone slabs and clay tablets, it describes the length of days and nights for an entire year and lists sixty-six constellations. It is also the earliest known star chart. Astrology subsequently spread to ancient Egypt and Greece, and then to the Roman Empire. Ancient Egyptian solar calendars, known as 'Nilotic calendars', appeared at the beginning of the third millennium BC. They traced the pattern of agricultural activities and the seasons. In fact, the Egyptians had noticed that with each appearance of Sirius in the sky, the annual flooding of the Nile was imminent. At the time, they used astronomical observation based on eclipses and the movements of the planets. The Celts, in turn, practised a form of astrology inspired by the power of trees. The Hindus, the Mayans and the Chinese had also developed systems to predict events based on celestial observation. In the Middle Ages, astrology was studied in universities, in the same way that meteorology, alchemy, astronomy, science and medicine were studied.

The Church did not question its existence, given that there were astrologer popes, particularly during the Renaissance, who examined the stars before making political or military decisions. However, astrology was separated from astronomy during the Enlightenment, which led to its decline. In the nineteenth century, it survived in small private circles, only to reappear today and again arouse new interest through the skills of erudite researchers.

Deciphering the sky

Astrology was sustained by the knowledge gained in astronomy and the two disciplines were inseparable. Need we remind you that most of the great astronomers were also astrologers? Hence, a person's birth chart is made up of astronomical calculations. It takes the form of a star chart containing many symbols, and it is the astrologer's task to decipher it. In what resembles a hieroglyphic cartouche, it tells the story of a person's life, with all its joys and sorrows, from birth to death.

The twelve signs of the zodiac

The zodiac allows us to perceive what cannot be seen; it is a record of the history of the world and the life of humankind written in the star-studded sky. The word is derived from the Greek *zodiakos*, which means a 'circle of little animals'. It is represented as a belt that surrounds Earth through which the planets transit at different speeds. It corresponds to the band of sky on both sides of the ecliptic, the path along which the sun,

MAI.
JUNI.
III
IV
LIEBIG
COMPANY'S
FLEISCH-EXTRACT.
ZWILLINGE.
KREBS.
Herzliche Liebe verband die
Zwillinge Castor und Pollux;
Götterhuld weihte zum Preis, ihnen
das Sternbild dafür.
Der
Thierkreis
„Krebs, verletze den Herakles,
tödtend die Hyder" spricht Here, die
zum Lohne den Krebs dann in den
Thierkreis erhebt.
Siehe Rückseite.

moon and main planets of the solar system travel. The ecliptic traverses thirteen recognizable groups of stars, referred to as constellations.

In astrology, the zodiac is divided into twelve zones associated with twelve signs; the thirteenth, known as Ophiuchus 'the snake bearer', is not used. The signs still bear the names that were given to their corresponding constellations 2,000 years ago: Aries, Taurus, Gemini, Cancer, Leo, Virgo, Libra, Scorpio, Sagittarius, Capricorn, Aquarius and Pisces. Owing to the phenomenon known as precession of the equinoxes, there is a one-month delay between the sign of the zodiac for a given period and the corresponding constellation appearing in the sky. Therefore, a person's sign refers to the position of the sun at the moment of birth. Astrologers can find all the positions of the planets they use to create birth charts in ephemerides, tables that indicate the positions of Mercury, Venus, Mars, Jupiter, Saturn, Uranus, Neptune and Pluto, and the two luminaries, the sun and the moon, until 2050.

Whether it is considered a science, a philosophy or a school of thought, astrology remains a discipline that helps us to gain a better understanding of ourselves.

HIPPOCRATES: THE TEMPERAMENT THEORY

A brief history

Hippocrates was born in about 460 BC on the Greek island of Cos and died in around 370 BC in Larissa. He is considered the father of medicine and set down the ethical standards of his discipline through more than sixty works compiled in the *Hippocratic Corpus*. His Temperament Theory is still considered relevant for astrology. It describes four types of individuals according to the notion of 'humours': when fire is the ruling element of a chart, it produces a choleric or bilious temperament, linked to the muscular system; when earth is the ruling element, it produces a melancholic or nervous temperament, linked to the nervous system; when air is the ruling element, it produces a sanguine or cheerful temperament, linked to the respiratory system; and finally, when water is the ruling element, it produces a phlegmatic or calm temperament, linked to the digestive system. Hippocrates believed there was a clear connection between the language of the stars and medicine in the broadest sense. He was convinced that illness had meaning and associated the art of healing with astrology. He considered it the astrologer's role to help patients find the psychosomatic origin of their illness in order to find healing. By studying a birth chart, an individual's sensitivity to certain health problems could be discerned. Therefore, better self-knowledge allowed patients to improve and overcome their difficulties.

HIPPOCRATE
CHOCOLAT GUÉRIN-BOUTRON
HIPPOCRATE, 460 ans avant notre ère, découvre les premiers remèdes et mérite d'être appelé le père de la médecine.
LES BIENFAITEURS DE L'HUMANITÉ
84 Sujets variés

PYTHAGORAS: TOWARDS RATIONAL ASTROLOGY

A brief history

Born on the island of Samos in about 570 BC, Pythagoras became a philosopher before leaving Greece to study astronomy and geometry in Egypt. He was also a religious reformer and a pre-Socratic philosopher. He likened the cosmos to a lyre whose strings vibrate and produce sounds. He also gave a mystical interpretation to numbers, by which he assigned a number to each thing and drew a correspondence between them and the mechanisms of nature. The discovery of the golden ratio is attributed to him. Pythagoras thought the world was built in a particular order, 'a macrocosm and microcosm, as above, so below, hence the whole'. He gave it a geometrical structure based on calculations to find its rhythms and harmonies. This great mathematician spent eight years in Mesopotamia, where he studied astrology and developed it further. He was convinced that humankind and the planets were interdependent, and he demonstrated that all stars have a life and intelligence of their own. He brought about a change in the approach to astrology because he was convinced that people should be masters of their own destiny and no longer subject to the law of the gods. By demonstrating free will in humans, astrology ceased to be fatalistic. Following the work done by Pythagoras, the Greeks took a more rational approach to astrology.

2

PYTHAGORAS CLAR OLYMP. 64

Pythagoras samius laudasse silentia fertur
Pythagoræ uera est numquit imago: tacet

PTOLEMY: A SCIENTIFIC APPROACH

A brief history

Claudius Ptolemy was born around the year 100 and died in about 170 in Canopus, Egypt. A resident of Alexandria, this mathematician, astronomer, astrologer and geographer endeavoured to elucidate the physical laws of nature. He is regarded as one of the fathers of modern astrology and drew up horoscopes and published books which are still references today: *Almagest*, an astronomical compendium containing a catalogue of 1,022 stars, and *Tetrabiblos*, an encyclopedia of ancient astrological knowledge. He also established an astronomical law, the 'precession of the equinoxes', and he codified the four elementary qualities: hot, cold, dry and wet. He practised tropical astrology, which is linked to the seasons. He rightly believed that astrology should consider a number of factors, such as country, education and environment, as they influence the person in the same way as the position of the planets on the day of birth. In the introduction to the *Tetrabiblos*, Ptolemy explains the difference between astronomy and astrology: 'The one, first alike in order and in power, leads to the knowledge of the figurations of the sun, the moon and the stars; and of their relative aspects to each other, and to the earth: the other takes into consideration the changes which their aspects create, by means of their natural properties, in objects under their influence.' This exemplifies his highly scientific approach to astrology.

VÉRITABLE EXTRAIT DE VIANDE LIEBIG.
Astronomes célèbres.
Claude Ptolémée.
2.
Reproduction interdite.
Voir l'explication au verso.

NOSTRADAMUS: CLAIRVOYANCE AND ASTROLOGY

A brief history

Michel de Nostredame, known as Nostradamus, was born on 14 December 1503 (Julian calendar) in Saint-Rémy-de-Provence and died on 2 July 1566 in Salon-de-Provence. As an apothecary, he was interested in making natural herbal remedies. However, he discovered astrology in the course of travels through France between 1540 and 1545, and later in Italy between 1547 and 1549, which led him to write almanacs. His zodiac sign was Capricorn, the sign that represents time. He published his prophecies in the form of four-line verses or quatrains *The Centuries*, through which he described future events up to the year 3797. In order to do this, he used the great conjunctions, planetary and chronological periods, and his own gift of clairvoyance. When his prophecies were published in 1555, they were a great success, especially after he had predicted the tragic death of King Henry II of France on 10 July 1559. He then became astrologer to Henry's widow, Catherine de' Medici, who also appointed him physician and adviser to her son, King Charles IX, in 1564. His birth chart reveals his personality: the sun and Mercury in Capricorn indicated his precision and great perseverance; the Moon in Scorpio highlighted his appetite for inquiry; Uranus in Pisces defined his gift of clairvoyance; and Jupiter in Cancer was behind his great memory and his success in many fields.

Dieu se sert icy de ma bouche
Pour t'anoncer la verité,
Si ma prediction te touche
Rends grace à sa Divinité.

J. Sauvé sculp.

THE ASTROLOGICAL PLANETS
The planets

The zodiac can be likened to a celestial highway on which all the planets travel as they appear to revolve around the earth. If we compare it to a motorway, fast-moving heavenly bodies – such as the moon, Mercury, Venus and Mars – are sports cars, while slow-moving planets – such as Saturn, Jupiter, Uranus, Neptune and Pluto – are heavy goods vehicles. By consulting ephemerides, we can locate the position of the planets by longitude and latitude on any given day. Each planet has qualities, significance and influence depending on the sign and the house where it is found, the individual and the events in their life. This solar system is ordered by a number of very specific laws. The planets transit on a plane very close to the ecliptic, inside the band we know as the zodiac. They orbit in the same direction around the sun, but at different speeds and in different periods, according to the following principles: the closer a planet is to the sun, the faster it travels and the shorter its orbital period. Jupiter is the largest planet and Mercury is the smallest. Mercury, Venus, Mars, Jupiter and Saturn can all be seen with the naked eye. However, Uranus, Neptune and Pluto cannot. Because it is close to the Sun and glows red, Mercury is always difficult to observe, while Mars is recognizable by its red colour. The rings of Saturn, a duller planet, can be made out through binoculars.

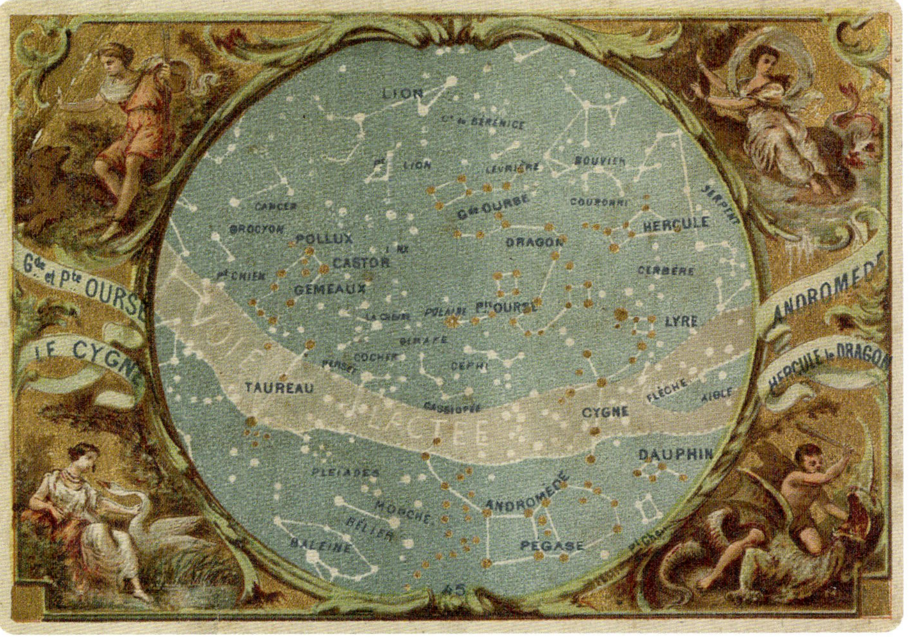

Gde et Pte OURSE
LE CYGNE
ANDROMEDE
HERCULE le DRAGON
LION
Cne de BÉRÉNICE
Pt LION
LEVRIÈRE
BOUVIER
SERPENT
CANCER
PROCYON
POLLUX
CASTOR
Gd OURSE
COURONNE
HERCULE
DRAGON
Pt CHIEN
GÉMEAUX
CERBÈRE
POLAIRE
Pte OURSE
LYRE
LA CHÈVRE
GIRAFE
COCHER
PERSÉE
CÉPHÉE
TAUREAU
CASSIOPÉE
VOIE LACTÉE
CYGNE
FLÈCHE
AIGLE
DAUPHIN
PLEIADES
ANDROMÈDE
MOUCHE
BÉLIER
BALEINE
PÉGASE
45

THE SUN, SELF-AWARENESS

The planets

In all mythologies, the sun is the giver of energy and power. The symbol of life, it is worshipped as the god of light, arts, divination and music. For the ancient Egyptians he was Ra; for the Greeks, Helios; and for the Romans, Apollo. The first of the two luminaries (the other being the moon, the heavenly body of the night), the sun determines our star sign, where it remains for about 30 days. It takes twelve months for the sun to traverse the zodiac. It rules the sign of Leo. The sun stands for vitality, radiance and generosity. In one chart, it represents the figure of the father, husband, boss and the authority; and for a woman, it represents her relationship with her husband and the type of man she is looking for. It symbolizes maturity between the ages of thirty-five and forty. It provides information on personality, self-awareness and ambition. Where society is concerned, the sun represents the state, institutions, public authorities and monarchy. As regards health, it rules over the heart, spine and solar plexus, and general vitality. It symbolizes career, honours, reputation, vocation and ambition. The sun expresses the power of the person, our ability to be autonomous and our will. It is associated with our highest aspirations, our ideals. Individuals governed by the sun exert a powerful positive influence on the people around them. Their attitude is loyal, courageous and protective. They are ambitious, self-willed and have a sense of leadership.

Cie LIEBIG.
O SOLEIL
DIAMÈTRE 1.387.600 KILOM.
DISTANCE 148.670.000 KILOM.
VOIR AU VERSO.

THE MOON, THE INNER LIFE

The planets

In Greek mythology, the moon is personified as Selene. Her face is immaculate white. The other heavenly bodies pale when she rides her silver chariot across the sky every night to visit her lover, who lies in a deep sleep. After the sun, the moon is the other important luminary for the interpretation of a birth chart. The moon's cycle lasts an average of twenty-nine days. It moves quickly and only stays in each sign for two or three days. The sign of Cancer is ruled by the moon. The moon stands for the inner personality, the world of the unconscious, all that is transitory, daily life, dreams and states of mind. It represents imagination, memory, sensitivity, receptivity, crowds, birth and the cycles of life. It also symbolizes the figure of the mother and wife, and the maternal qualities, fertility and children. For a man, the moon represents the way he 'experienced' his mother and the type of woman he is looking for; for a woman, it represents her relationship with her children and her family. The moon influences everyday life, mood, receptivity. Individuals governed by the moon have a nature that is gentle, devoted, sensitive and refined. Their character is peaceful and conciliatory. They have a creative temperament. Having well-developed maternal or paternal instincts, they like to be surrounded by the warmth of their home and family. Their inner lives are subject to their emotions and sensitivity. They are cyclical and tend to be at the mercy of their moods.

Cie. LIEBIG.
LONDON
C LUNE
DIAMÈTRE 3.480 KILOM.
DISTANCE 384.420 KILOM.
RÉVOLUTION 27 JOURS 7H. 43 M.
VOIR AU VERSO.

MERCURY, LANGUAGE

The planets

In Greek mythology, Mercury is personified as Hermes, a young man with winged feet who serves as the messenger of Olympus. He is an intermediary between the gods and humans. He is the protector of the shepherds and the guide of souls as they leave the earth. This planet is the closest to the sun and its orbit takes eighty days. It spends about a month in each sign. Mercury rules curious and communicative Gemini, and orderly and methodical Virgo. In one chart, it represents intellectual abilities, communication, speech, writing, study, commerce and short-distance travel. It symbolizes the age of adolescence and youth. People governed by Mercury keep their youthful appearance for a long time. As regards health, Mercury rules over the nerves, arms and hands. It represents the figure of the brother and the student, and the bonds that unite people through the tools of communication. The world of publishing, journalism, social networks, means of transport and travel are all associated with Mercury. Individuals ruled by this planet are characterized by their ability to communicate, quick-wittedness, sense of humour, ability to adapt to all situations, unceasing curiosity, perspicacity and eloquence. Because they are constantly in motion, they can easily take on too much. They have a talent for business and perform several activities at once.

Cie LIEBIG.
☿ MERCURE
DIAMÈTRE 4.900 KILOM.
DISTANCE 57.550.000 KILOM.
RÉVOLUTION 2 MOIS, 7 JOURS, 23 H. 15 M.
VOIR AU VERSO.

VENUS, DESIRES

The planets

In Greek mythology, Venus is personified by Aphrodite, the goddess of love, beauty and fertility. She is one of the twelve gods of Olympus. Close to the sun, Venus takes about 225 days to orbit the star. It spends about a month in each sign. Venus rules the signs of Libra and Taurus. It is the planet of charm, sensuality and seduction. It symbolizes the age of fifteen, the awakening of feelings and the first emotions of love. For a woman, Venus shows how to be seductive. For a man, it indicates the way he expects to be loved and how to express his feelings. Venus represents the figure of the sister, wife and lover. It symbolizes balance, all that is pleasant, love, the arts, creativity and happiness. Individuals ruled by Venus are very sensual and highly conciliatory, and seek their own comfort, well-being and tranquillity. As regards health, Venus rules over the female sexual organs, hormonal function and the endocrine system. It also defines the way in which people express their feelings and emotions. It stands for gentleness and emotional ties, as well as the artistic and aesthetic domains, and culture and the arts. People governed by Venus are seductive and pleasant-natured; they have deep and sincere feelings and wear their heart on their sleeve. They are drawn to pleasures and lofty ideals, and seek harmony in everything they undertake.

Cie LIEBIG.
♀ VÉNUS
DIAMÈTRE 12.603 KILOM.
DISTANCE 107.535.000 KILOM.
RÉVOLUTION 7 MOIS 14 JOURS 16H. 49 M.
VOIR AU VERSO.

MARS, ACTION

The planets

In Greek mythology, Mars is personified as Ares, the god of war and the struggle of battle. He is portrayed as a destructive, violent god, but also the protector of the harvest. He also embodies justice, courage and positive strength. This planet is similar in size to the earth and spends between forty-five and sixty days in a sign. It takes about 687 days to orbit the sun. Mars rules the signs of Aries and Scorpio. As the planet of energy, it symbolizes action and is at the root of any initiative. It represents courage, the sense of struggle, sport, passion, conquest and combativeness. It symbolizes the strength that comes with age, people between the ages of thirty and forty - the period when ambitions are realized - and the figure of a spouse in general and a lover for a woman. For a man, it denotes his virility, spirit of conquest and the way he asserts himself; for a woman, it teaches her how to act and use her Yang side. Individuals ruled by Mars are dynamic, open, direct and spontaneous. They have strong instincts. In this respect, the presence of Mars in a sign indicates a degree of aggressiveness. Moreover, people governed by Mars are endowed with an excellent physique. As regards health, Mars rules over the muscular system, inflammatory disorders, the gallbladder and the head. People ruled by Mars are strong-willed, sparing no effort to boldly and clearly fulfil their goals by overcoming all obstacles. They are fiercely independent.

Cie LIEBIG
♂ MARS
DIAMÈTRE 6.735 KILOM.
DISTANCE 226.520.000 KILOM.
RÉVOLUTION 1 AN 10 MOIS 21 JOURS 17 H. 22 M.
VOIR AU VERSO.

JUPITER, THE SENSE OF ORGANIZATION

The planets

The symbol of Jupiter is an eagle with outstretched wings. In Greek mythology, Jupiter is personified by Zeus, the master of Olympus who reigns over the earth, the sky, mankind and other gods. He symbolizes appeasement, wisdom, justice and victory. The first of the 'slow' planets, Jupiter spends about a year in each sign and its orbit around the Sun takes twelve years. It rules the sign of Sagittarius. In astrology, it is considered the 'Great Benefactor'. It symbolizes law, justice and religion, but also education, success, wealth, generosity and games. It represents luck, optimism, enjoyment of life, extroversion, benevolence, generosity and authority. From an occupational standpoint, it governs the professions, such as those in banking, justice and academia, and work involving racehorses. It is an expansive planet that shows individuals how to position themselves on a material and social level. As regards health, it rules over the liver, thighs and blood. Jupiter is synonymous with protection. Individuals ruled by Jupiter are open, spontaneous, loyal and jovial. They have a sense of moderation, organization, easy assimilation and a keen sense of judgement. They are also conservative. They have a certain predilection for speculating and are quite lucky in business. Their enthusiasm and sociability allow them to excel at diplomacy.

Cie LIEBIG.
♃ JUPITER
DIAMÈTRE 143.800 KILOM.
DISTANCE 773.480.000 KILOM.
RÉVOLUTION 11 ANS 10 MOIS 17 JOURS 8 H 42 M.
VOIR AU VERSO.

SATURN, PENCHANT FOR POWER

The planets

In Greek mythology, Saturn is personified by Cronus, the son of Uranus. He is the god of time and destiny. His main fear was to lose power. After being exiled by his son Jupiter, he cultivated wisdom, peace and justice. Saturn is the last planet that can be seen with the naked eye and is the ruler of the sign of Capricorn. It takes between twenty-nine and thirty years to orbit the sun, and it spends two and a half years in each sign. It represents the structure of personality, its foundations, depth of thought, concentration, limitations and inhibitions, and the passing of time and old age. It allows people to become aware of their responsibilities and to differentiate themselves. It represents the mature individual aged sixty and onwards, and it also symbolizes the figure of the father who provides protection and security. It symbolizes discipline, conservatism, austerity, wisdom, patience, responsibility, economy, precision and perseverance. It governs work, traditions, conservatism, agriculture and prisons. Saturn shows the way ahead, like a scout. As regards health, Saturn rules over the skin, skeleton and joints. The planet is consulted in a chart if information is required about erudition, the scientific mind, perseverance, capacity for work and the maturity of the person. Individuals ruled by Saturn are ambitious, thoughtful, introverted, calm and reserved. They remain calm and collected in any situation and give an impression of restraint and detachment.

Les jours de la semaine.
SATURDAY
SAMEDI.
SONNABEND
Véritable Extrait de viande LIEBIG.
Voir l'explication au verso.

URANUS, THE INVENTIVE MIND

The planets

The symbol for Uranus is 'H', the first letter of Herschel, the astronomer who discovered this planet on 13 March 1781. In Greek mythology, Uranus is the master of the heavens who, together with Gaia, sired the universe and brought the earth and humans out of Chaos, the void. The planet Uranus takes eighty-four years to orbit the sun and spends between seven and eight years in each sign. Uranus rules the sign of Aquarius and symbolizes freedom, independence, the unexpected and economic and social upheaval. It represents rapid change, awareness, waves, new technologies and cutting-edge inventions. It is associated with revolutions, progress and discoveries in every field. It is the planet of creativity, originality, non-conformism, altruism and independence. In a chart, Saturn indicates individuals' inventive faculties, the sudden and unexpected changes in their lives and their friendships. As regards health, it rules over nerve impulses, nerves, bodily fluids and the bloodstream. Uranus often announces a change in direction or in life at around the age of forty-two, when a person is freed from certain chains that hinder advancement. Individuals ruled by Uranus are altruistic, with a strong sense of fellowship, and they like to dedicate themselves to important environmental or humanitarian causes. Their innovative and sometimes extreme ideas may cause concern, but they are always constructive and ahead of their time.

URANUS
URANUS

NEPTUNE, SOURCES OF INSPIRATION

The planets

In Greek mythology, Neptune is personified by Poseidon, the god of the seas and rivers, and also metallurgy and sculpture. Poseidon's trident is traditionally used to represent the planet. Discovered in 1846, Neptune spends thirteen and a half years in each sign and takes about 165 years to orbit the sun. In astrology, it rules the sign of Pisces. It governs intuition, mysticism, the world of dreams, inspiration, the quest for an ideal, imagination, irrationality and religion, in addition to illusions, doubts, hidden things and the invisible world. Neptune also governs creativity and the artistic world. It represents the sea, water, poetry and music. As regards health, it rules over the psyche, food poisoning and drug intoxication, misdiagnosis, alcohol and drug addiction, the glands and feet. Individuals ruled by Neptune are very receptive to different situations and are empathetic and obliging. They are instilled with a spirit of charity, compassion and sacrifice. They live in tune with their emotions and intuitions. Their existence is often linked to a desire for union, mainly where love is concerned. Neptune is consulted in a chart to discover individuals' deepest aspirations and ideals. It also provides information about their imagination, creativity and spirituality. The major difficulty for people ruled by Neptune is to find their way through all their emotions and feelings.

LABBEY & Cie PARIS
Soieries, Lainages, Nouveautés élégantes
NEPTUNE
VALLET, MINOT & Cie 5 R. BÉRANGER, PARIS.

PLUTO, THE ABILITY TO TRANSFORM

The planets

In Greek mythology, Pluto is personified by Hades, the god of the dead, the underworld and precious metals. Recently discovered (1930), Pluto is the most distant planet in our solar system. It orbits the sun in 249 years and spends about twenty years in each sign. Pluto rules the sign of Scorpio which, like the phoenix, always rises from its ashes. It represents power, crowds and violence in the world. As regards health, Pluto rules over sexuality and related organs, and degenerative diseases. It goes back to the roots of the individual, to deep instincts. It is the innate, the unavoidable, the instinctive force that drives one to act. It asks questions about life, destiny and the meaning of existence. It represents metamorphosis and questioning. Its role is to bring an end to anything that does not allow individuals to progress and evolve. It is a planet of initiation, mutation and regeneration. It is associated with mysteries, secrets, mesmerism and the occult. It shows how individuals face their destiny, the great upheavals to be encountered and gain awareness. People ruled by Pluto are strong-willed and endowed with extreme power; they are leaders who influence those around them and know how to steer them. Pluto is consulted in a chart to know how individuals will find fulfilment in their lives through their continuous questioning.

32. Pluton.

THE HOUSES
Earthly domains

The first house, known as the ascendant or rising sign, covers our self-affirmation and the way in which we express ourselves and behave. It tells us about our appearance. The second house shows our material possessions and the money we earn and spend. The third house covers our siblings, primary or basic education, neighbourhood, means of communication and expression, intellect and short journeys. The fourth house, known as the Imum Coeli or 'bottom of the sky', covers our home, land, family and heredity, and represents the father. The fifth house covers our sentimental life, children, artistic creation, leisure and education. The sixth house governs work and daily life, health, minor illnesses and pets. The seventh house, known as the descendant, governs marriage, social life and contracts. It also represents the spouse. The eighth house rules over transformations, the occult, legacies, the end of life and sexuality. The ninth house symbolizes higher education, travel, other cultures and spiritual life. The tenth house, known as Medium Coeli or the Midheaven, tells us about our professional and public life, success and vocation. It also represents the mother. The eleventh house is the house of friendships, projects, customers, assistance and support. Finally, the twelfth house represents dedication, hardship, retirement, hidden things, chronic illness and loneliness. It also describes inner life and life in the womb.

THE FOUR ELEMENTS

The forces of nature

The signs of the zodiac are divided into four elements: fire, earth, air and water, each of which is analogous with three signs. When it comes to fire, Aries represents a brightly burning flame. Aries are fast and energetic, and they love to take the lead. Leo represents the sun's warmth. Leos command authority by their radiance. Sagittarius is a will-o'-the-wisp that rises and scatters. Sagittarians bring warmth and generosity to those around them. The earth signs are practical and uncompromising. Taurus represents tilled soil that is fertilized to become productive. Virgo is symbolized by loose-grained sand. Virgos take part in building things. Capricorn symbolizes rocks and mountains. Capricorns are strong and ambitious. Air signs are communicators. Gemini is symbolized by a light and fast-moving stream of air. Geminians express themselves through speech, writing and communication. Libra is a soft and pleasant breeze. The air is imbued with love, enchantment and harmony. Aquarius is symbolized by compressed air that is ready to explode, giving Aquarians a rebellious side. Water signs are intuitive and emotional. Cancer is likened to the water of a fast-flowing river. Cancerians' emotions are changeable. Scorpios are symbolized by the seemingly still waters of a lake. Scorpios evolve in a mysterious world under the surface. Pisces is represented by the waters of the oceans, with their ebb and flow. Pisceans allow themselves to be led by their intuition and their imagination.

SUCHARD
Chocolat SUCHARD

THE METEOROLOGY OF THE SIGNS

The seasons

In our part of the world, the twelve signs of the zodiac are closely tied to the four seasons. The three signs of spring (Aries, Taurus and Gemini) are dynamic and extroverted. Aries brings renewal with the arrival of good weather; in Taurus, the earth is fertile and seeds take root; in Gemini, the vegetation becomes lush. The three summer signs (Cancer, Leo and Virgo) are open, communicative and creative. Cancer coincides with the beginning of summer, when nature is at its peak; in Leo, the fruits are picked and the grain is harvested; and in Virgo, the crops are sorted. The signs of autumn (Libra, Scorpio and Sagittarius) form a link between two seasons. Libra balances the day with the night; Scorpio brings transformation of matter with the falling leaves; and Sagittarius is the time to prepare for the coming winter. These are signs of alteration and transformation. The signs of winter (Capricorn, Aquarius and Pisces) correspond to the period of latency. They have a rich inner life. The cardinal signs (Aries, Cancer, Libra and Capricorn) indicate the beginning of their season. They implement projects that benefit the community. The fixed signs (Taurus, Leo, Scorpio and Aquarius) mark the middle of their season. They have consistency and great stamina. And the mutable signs (Gemini, Virgo, Sagittarius, Pisces) come at the end of their season. They embody transition and movement. They are adaptable and obliging, and they like to express themselves.

IX
CACAO
CHOCOLAT SUCHARD

ARIES, A CONQUEROR

Spring sign

Aries, the constellation of the ram, is the sign of people born between 21 March and 20 April. Aries has fire as its element and is ruled by the planet Mars. Its lucky day is Tuesday and its lucky number is one. It has ruby as its stone, red as its colour and iron as its metal. Tulips are the favourite flowers of this sign. The symbol of Aries resembles a sprouting seed; however, if the fire is not stoked, it goes out. It also evokes a set of rams' horns, epitomizing the vitality and vigour of the sign. Its season is spring, a time in which darkness turns into light and the earth awakens from its slumber. Because of their active, exalted and impulsive nature, Aries can act with haste. Novelty arouses their enthusiasm. They need a lot of activities and find a day-to-day existence and routine boring. Because they are open, spontaneous and direct, Aries appreciate clear-cut situations. At times quick-tempered, Aries are fighters who will not hesitate to stand up for a cause. But they always fight fair. Aries are indomitable and independent conquerors flowing with life. When they need to say something, they are straightforward. There are two types of Aries. The first are outwardly orientated, extroverted and hyperactive, with a fully-fledged spirit of conquest, whereas the second are introverted and on an intellectual or spiritual quest. Individuals born under this sign must show perseverance and finish what they begin in order to achieve their goal and find fulfilment.

CHOCOLAT FELIX POTIN
MARS
LE BELIER
Les Giboulées

A SPONTANEOUS LOVER

Aries

Aries are quite impulsive. They often become very excited about something before quickly running out of breath. Their sign is one of conquest, adventure and spontaneous seduction. Aries are very direct at expressing their feelings and their love has a chivalrous nature. The other fire signs are suited to Aries because they share the same dynamic, energetic and enterprising nature. Aries are also perfectly matched with the air signs, mainly Aquarius. In fact, Aries are compatible with many signs when it comes to love. When two Aries come together, it is love at first sight: sparks will fly and their relationship will be scintillating. Aries and Taurus are complementary signs with the latter providing stability for the former. Aries and Geminians share the same lively spirit. The Aries and Cancer couple will have ups and downs. The latter's sensitivity can clash with the former's ardour. Aries and Leo are strong-willed signs. Both have an energetic and radiant temperament. Aries and Virgo also complement each other. Far-sighted and prudent Virgos have a calming effect on their partners' impulses. Aries cannot resist the charms of Librans and are aroused by Scorpios' mysterious nature. Sagittarian generosity moves them. Aries and Capricorns share common ambitions or passions, whereas Aries and Aquarians see the future the same way. And while Aries like clear-cut situations, Pisceans prefer them to be vague.

MARS
Serie 386 Nr. 3

ON A MISSION

Aries

Aries are incapable of staying still. Therefore, they need a career that keeps them on their feet and in constant renewal. They need to burn off their energy and to take the initiative. They are leaders who command authority. Their profession must allow them total freedom to act in order to preserve their independence. These spirited adventurers know how to take risks when necessary. They are fast and dynamic. But they also appreciate teamwork, as long as they are in charge. Aries have a sanguine temperament and can become enraged if things are not as they want them. They have a rather comprehensive view of things and prefer not to be hampered by the details. There is no stopping them when they act. Hyperactive Aries do not tolerate monotony and often change jobs several times during their career. Ambitious and determined, they endeavour to climb the ladder quickly. They are often found in positions of command in the army. They can also be found as police officers in the field, but also in the posts of company directors, managers and coaches, as top-level sportsmen and women, and in professions involving risk-taking or adventure, such as that of a special correspondent. They also choose professions that require creativity, such as in advertising, audiovisual communication and architecture. Aries are excellent in business because of their superb sense of negotiation.

MARS
Le premier Soleil.
HUNTLEY & PALMERS
BISCUITS
Reading & London
Le Bélier

JASON AND THE GOLDEN FLEECE

Aries

Jason, the son of King Aeson of Iolcus, was still a child when he was hidden in the mountains for his safety. When the young prince reached adulthood, he claimed his father's throne from his uncle Pelias. But the usurper refused and challenged him to bring back the Golden Fleece of the sacred ram of the king of Colchis. To do this, Jason embarked on a ship, *Argo*, with a crew that included Atalanta the huntress, Heracles and the twins Castor and Pollux. Before he set sail, the goddess Athena bestowed him with an oak branch for his protection. After a number of adventures, Jason arrived in Colchis to collect the famous trophy. The king of this place, Aeëtes, allowed him to take the Golden Fleece if he succeeded in ploughing a field with two fire-breathing bulls and sowing dragon teeth. With help from a magic potion prepared by Medea, the daughter of Aeëtes who had fallen in love with him, Jason accomplished his mission and overcame all dangers. Together with Medea, he retrieved the Golden Fleece after killing the winged ram Chrysomallos. Upon his return, Jason took back his father's throne. This myth reflects the Aries personality, which is valiant, loyal and belligerent. This sign loves a challenge. The fleece represents the strength and power of Aries. In the myth, the sacrifice of the ram symbolizes the overcoming of fear, essential to the success of the missions undertaken by Aries, who will go to the very end to accomplish them.

LA SPEDIZIONE DEGLI ARGONAUTI.

6. Il rapimento del veto d'oro custodito dal drago.

FRAGONARD, A FIERY TEMPERAMENT

Aries

Jean Honoré Fragonard was born on 5 April 1732 in Grasse and died on 22 August 1806 in Paris. He was one of the leading painters in eighteenth-century France. His parents took him from his native Provence at the age of six to settle in Paris. The child showed his artistic talents at an early age and received his first lessons from Chardin, a painter known for his still life and genre paintings and work in pastels. He continued his apprenticeship in the studio of François Boucher. At the age of twenty (1752), after quickly mastering his art, he won the Prix de Rome, a scholarship that allowed him to travel through Italy. He later returned to Paris and gained the recognition of the royal court. In 1769, he married Marie-Anne Gérard, also a painter, and had two children. His sensual and graceful canvases reveal his great technical virtuosity. One of his best-known works is *Young Girl Reading*. In his birth chart, the sun, Mercury and Saturn in the sign of Aries, the moon in Leo and Mars and Uranus in Sagittarius signify a fiery temperament. A very energetic and ambitious man, Fragonard always endeavoured to be the best at everything he undertook. He was endowed with a great capacity for work and was a perfectionist in his art. In order to stand out, he wanted to bring his own personal style to the art of painting. Venus in Taurus indicates a strong and exacting form of sensuality and a highly inspired artistic sensibility.

MUSÉE DU LOUVRE
L'INSPIRATION
Ecole Française. Fragonard.

TAURUS, A PEACEFUL ROMANTIC

Spring sign

Taurus, the constellation of the bull, is the sign of people born between 21 April and 20 May. Taurus has earth as its element and is ruled by the planet Venus. Its lucky day is Friday and its lucky number is two. It has emerald as its stone, green as its colour and copper as its metal. Roses are the favourite flowers of this sign. Its symbol depicts an animal's head with horns or a cup resting on it. Taureans have finely tuned senses. Their sense of smell is their main form of perception. Endowed with a huge capacity for work, they are able to sustain their effort and enjoy long-term tasks. They are realistic, pragmatic, headstrong and mighty, and see everything through to the end. They are steady and stubborn. Taurus is the sign of the builder. It is also one of peace and is close to nature and animals. Taureans like to live in a healthy, serene and comfortable environment. They are hedonistic and appreciate quality food. Highly sensual, they are romantic, sentimental, possessive – even jealous – and faithful. They react slowly because they like to take their time. They are creatures of habit. They are materialistic and have a sense of ownership. Taureans are tranquil; it takes a lot to rile them. Consequently, their outbursts of anger are always unexpected and bitter. They are very artistic and creative, and are often proficient singers and artists. There are two types of Taureans: the first are conservative, set in their ways and seek security; the second are determined, energetic and always ready to fight.

CHOCOLAT MASSON _ PARIS
AVRIL
LE TAUREAU
Les Œufs de Pâques

A CHARMER

Taurus

Taureans are refined and lovers of beauty. They are sentimental, romantic and charming, and they are charmers. The earth and water signs, particularly Cancer, are a good fit. Preferring simple and caring relationships, they look for genuinely loving and steady relationships. Taureans are compatible with Aries, who take them away from their routine. In return, Taureans calm their partners' all-conquering nature and allow them to unwind. Two Taureans together bring out each other's hedonistic side and enjoy life. Taureans balance Geminians, whose desire for change can, however, push them away. Sensuality, patience and gentleness unite Taurus and Cancer. As for Leos, they are attracted by Taurean charm and sensuality. Virgos appeal to Taureans with their calmness, gentleness, charm and practicality. Librans and Taureans share their sensuality and the desire to please. That way they continuously give each other pleasure. On the other hand, a Taurus-Scorpio union can sometimes be stormy. But is it not true that opposites attract? Taureans appreciate Sagittarians' dynamic and enterprising nature, which they find reassuring. Taureans and Capricornians, who share a love of possessions, quickly look for a cosy little nest to settle in. Taureans are captivated by the genius and originality of Aquarians. And where a Piscean is concerned, Taureans will take care of every detail, allowing their partner to go with the flow. The carnal attraction between them is very strong.

Serie 366 Nr. 4

AN INNATE ADMINISTRATOR

Taurus

Taureans tend to seek a stable job in business or in the creative industries or the arts. They are objective, realistic and patient. Endowed with a great capacity for work, they see everything through to the end, even if it takes a long time to achieve their goals. Their action plans are always effective and their career choices are well thought out. They change direction very little during the course of their career. They are reassured by a certain amount of routine. They make excellent team leaders as they are good listeners. Taureans often choose artistic professions ruled by Venus, such as dancing, singing, hairdressing, fashion and perfumery. Occupations associated with the land, animals and nature also appeal to them. As a result, many are farmers, agronomists, winemakers, landscapers, horticulturists, gardeners and forest wardens. Taureans also like to build. They often work in the building trade, as architects, builders or engineers. As they are fond of food and have refined tastes, they also turn to the catering trades and professions, such as those of chef or restaurateur. Performance-oriented and highly efficient, Taureans show at an early age their desire to make and earn money, in order to guarantee their material security and a certain level of comfort. They possess a keen sense of smell, a good nose for business and organization skills. They excel in the field of finance as bankers and asset managers.

GEBOREN ZWISCHEN
21. APRIL U. 20. MAI.
Die Stier-Menschen
Sie sind das Urbild stolzer Kraft,
Erfolg ist ihr Begehr,
Das Große, was ihr Geist erschafft
Fällt ihnen garnicht schwer.
Sie lieben Kunst und frohen Sinn,
Geselligkeit, Humor,
Doch oftmals kommt auch Eigensinn
In ihrem Leben vor.
GLÜCKSTEINE: ACHAT
GLÜCKFARBEN: GELB

THESEUS AND THE MINOTAUR

Taurus

Upon falling in love with beautiful Europa, the daughter of King Agenor, Zeus changed himself into a superb white bull in order to seduce her. After she climbed on his back, he took her away to Crete. Minos was born from their union and became the king of Crete. He later angered Poseidon, who sought revenge by making the queen, Pasiphaë, fall in love and mate with a white bull. This unnatural act produced the Minotaur, a hideous monster with the body of a man and the head of a bull. A humiliated Minos then imprisoned the animal in a labyrinth designed by Daedalus. However, in order to calm the monster's rage and hunger, he had to feed the monster seven Athenian boys and seven Athenian girls every year. To free his city from paying this awful tribute, Theseus, the son of the king of Athens, decided to kill the animal. He entered the labyrinth, killed the Minotaur and, with the help of a ball of string given to him by Ariadne, Minos's daughter who was in love with him, he found his way back. The victorious hero then escaped with her. This myth symbolizes Taureans' mastery of their instincts and their ability to transform their strength and power into fruitful creativity. They are constant, remaining true to their choices and promises. Because the sign is ruled by Venus, their purpose is to seek a fulfilling emotional experience such as that of Ariadne and Theseus.

THÉSÉE.

3. - Combat avec le Minotaure.

SHAKESPEARE, DESTINED TO SUCCEED

Taurus

William Shakespeare was born on 23 April 1564 (Julian calendar) and died on 23 April 1616 in Stratford-upon-Avon, England. His father was a leather merchant and his mother came from a wealthy Catholic family, and he seems to have had a formal education in the classics. Little is known about his life, except that he married Anne Hathaway, eight years his senior, at the age of eighteen. The couple had three children, and the death of his eleven-year-old son was to affect him for the rest of his life. Nothing more is known of him between 1585 and 1592, when he appeared in London as a budding actor and writer. In 1594, he joined the Lord Chamberlain's Men theatre company and performed for the royal court. He was a poet, playwright and writer, with a great mastery of poetic and literary forms. His plays are an extraordinary depiction of human nature and include characters from the different social classes. His best-known plays are *Macbeth*, *Hamlet*, *Othello* and *Romeo and Juliet*. The sun in Taurus in his birth chart meant that he was capable of achieving great social success. He felt powerful passion and was constantly in search of love. Venus and Neptune in Gemini gave him his ease in the literary field, thanks to his boundless imagination and powerful creative inspiration. Pluto in Pisces highlighted his fascination for mystery, intrigue and the intangible, while Uranus in Sagittarius offered the 'Bard of Avon' worldwide fame.

SHAKSPEARE
HAMLET

GEMINI, A HIGH-SPIRITED HARLEQUIN

Spring sign

Gemini, the constellation of the twins, is the sign of people born between 21 May and 21 June. Gemini has air as its element and is ruled by the planet Mercury. Its lucky day is Wednesday and its lucky number is three. It has blue topaz as its stone, turquoise as its colour and mercury as its metal. Peonies are the favourite flowers of this sign. The symbol for Gemini is two horizontal lines, symbolizing space, and two vertical lines, representing time. Geminians are fast, lively, active and changeable. This sign governs the fields of ideas, teaching, communication, travel, mobility and the world of adolescence. Being a dual sign, Geminians are truly elusive, like chameleons. They should avoid taking on too much and learn to settle down and concentrate. Geminians are divided into two types by temperament. Those with a 'Castor' temperament are distinguished by their great liveliness. Always in search of new sensations and on the move, they cannot stay put. They live in the moment. They have heightened sensitivity and emotions, love to travel and, on an emotional level, flit from one person to another for a long time before finding their rare gem. On the other hand, those with a 'Pollux' temperament are calm and control their emotions. They have powerful thoughts. Born entertainers, they are endowed with a sense of humour and enjoyment of life. Calculating, opportunistic, skilful and inventive, they also have a practical mind. They prefer a mundane life to solitude.

SUCHARD
Chocolat "SUCHARD"

THE KING OF SMOOTH TALKERS

Gemini

Like a dragonfly, Geminians flitter where the wind takes them. They often mix love with friendship. They prefer to be spontaneous and live in the moment. When it comes to love, they appreciate flirting and games. Their acting skills enable them to adapt to any situation. While we are left thinking they have found their mate, they are already off on another conquest. Their youthful spirit arouses the interest of Aries, who bring their sensual ardour. Their intelligence can weary Taureans, who seek an emotional relationship based on sensuality. But when they are very close, two Geminians together are constantly entertained. And because they are also highly imaginative, they feed Cancerian creativity. Their enjoyment of life and intellect appeal to Leos. Virgos, however, only appreciate the Geminian sense of humour in small doses. Geminians and Librans share their optimism and their interpersonal skills. Scorpios seek a deep and stable relationship, but a Geminian partner whose character is always changing cannot provide them with one. Sagittarians and Geminians, who are both very open-minded, are compatible through their taste for adventure. The serious, conventional and ambitious Capricorn can be won over by a versatile and light-hearted Geminian, but will eventually tire. Curiosity, intellect and communication connect Aquarius with Gemini. Fun-loving Geminians, who like being surrounded by many friends, are the opposite of Pisceans, who prefer peace and quiet.

GALERIES RÉMOISES
REIMS
CHAMPENOIS & Cie, PARIS.

THE ULTIMATE PEOPLE PERSON

Gemini

Geminians need movement, change, fantasy and contact. They excel at public relations. They need to move and constantly adapt in their jobs, otherwise boredom sets in. Being skilful and clever, Geminians know how to seize good opportunities when they arise. They are endowed with a great spirit of initiative and can have a thousand ideas at the same time. The important thing is for them to channel their overflowing mental energy. They have a gift for writing, a great sense of humour and instantaneous understanding, and they take an interest in everything. They like to express themselves and to teach. Geminians are the ultimate people persons. As they are good-natured and versatile, they also adapt to any situation and to all the people they meet. They appreciate teamwork and have a strong collaborative spirit. They are very creative and very skilled with their hands. They can move from one job to another depending on their aspirations and desires. However, they are not keen on long-term undertakings and prefer to finish the job quickly. As a result, they sometimes lack perseverance. Geminians are suited to the occupations of shopkeepers and sales representatives, and those of the entertainment industry, such as television hosts, comedians, humorists and actors. They are also found in professions associated with communication and justice, such as lawyers, teachers, social workers, athletes, writers, translators, interpreters and journalists.

Mois de Marie.

CASTOR AND POLLUX

Gemini

Castor and Pollux were the twin sons of Queen Leda, although they had different fathers. The former was mortal, the son of King Tyndarus; while the latter was immortal, fathered by Zeus, who had turned himself into a swan in order to seduce his mother. The twins were highly skilled and each gained mastery in a particular field: Pollux was a wrestler and Castor was a fine horseman. They were both inquisitive and wanted to learn all about life. They took part in the Argonauts' expedition to bring back the Golden Fleece. They fell in love with two sisters, with Castor marrying Hileira and Pollux marrying Phoebe. They were both practical jokers and liked to amuse themselves. However, when Castor was killed in a fight, Pollux was heartbroken and begged his father Zeus to let him join his beloved brother in the underworld, or else to make them both immortal. Zeus granted his wish by allowing the brothers to spend half the year with him on Mount Olympus and the other half in Hades. The twins were finally raised to the heavens and became the constellation of Gemini. They were made the protectors of Rome and the patron of sailors. This myth embodies the features of this sign: eternal adolescence, camaraderie, fantasy, a carefree attitude, enjoyment, curiosity, the spirit of discovery and mobility. Individuals ruled by this sign adapt to all situations. They have an innate sense of camaraderie. They are searching for their double, which is really the part of themselves they are missing.

CHOCOLAT IBLED
Paris. Mondicourt
LES GÉMEAUX
CASTOR ET POLLUX.
Castor et
Pollux, fils de Jupiter
et de Léda, Modèle
de l'amitie _ Placés
au Ciel à cause
de leur Union.

WAGNER, A DUAL-FACETED MAESTRO

Gemini

Richard Wagner was born on 22 May 1813 in Leipzig, Germany, and died on 13 February 1883 in Venice. His father, a city official, died six months after his birth. In August 1814, his mother remarried the actor Ludwig Geyer, whom Wagner would claim to be his real father. Under his stepfather's influence, Wagner fell in love with poetry and theatre at an early age. This nineteenth-century German composer is considered a great music theorist and his operas important works of lyric drama. The most famous are *Tristan and Isolde*, *The Ring of the Nibelung*, *The Flying Dutchman* and *Lohengrin*. His Geminian temperament led him to lead a bohemian and fantasy-filled life worthy of the hero of a novel. By becoming a destitute revolutionary and fugitive, a confidant of King Ludwig II of Bavaria, a music critic and an intellectual, he combined all the Geminian traits, accentuated by his rising sign, which was also Gemini. The sun conjunct Venus in his birth chart was a sign of his sensitivity towards women. They gave him comfort, help and advice throughout his life. In fact, he created superb heroines who portrayed women as sublime beings. The moon in Aquarius indicated original and avant-garde inspiration: he revolutionized opera by bringing together music, poetry, dance, painting and imitation in a single work.

BERÜHMTE COMPONISTEN.
RICHARD WAGNER.
geb. 22. Mai 1813 zu Dresden,
† 13. Februar 1883 zu Venedig.
„NIBELUNGENRING." „TANNHÄUSER".
„LOHENGRIN".
LIEBIG COMPANY'S FLEISCH-EXTRACT.

CANCER, GENTLE DREAMERS

Summer sign

Cancer, the constellation of the crab, is the sign of people born between 22 June and 22 July. Cancer has water as its element and is ruled by the moon. Its lucky day is Monday and its lucky number is 4. It has moonstone as its stone, white as its colour and silver as its metal. Dahlias are the favourite flowers of this sign. Its symbol resembles the number sixty-nine turned on its side, representing introversion and intimacy. It evokes gestation and life inside an egg. Cancer symbolizes the power of memory, heredity, family, maternal instinct and the land of birth. It also represents the world of early childhood. This sign is sensitive, emotional, irritable and very receptive to different situations. Cancerians are naturally anxious and need reassurance and security. They are dependent on their emotional relationships. And when they feel hurt, they retreat into their shell. While tenacious and persevering, they are also imaginative dreamers. They choose their relationships according to the impression they receive. They have an excellent memory. They are drawn to the past, history and literature for their hobbies and careers. There are two types of Cancerians. The first are homelovers and have deep ties to their roots, past, memories and habits. Typically melancholy, they seek a quiet existence and stable material well-being. The second have a nervous temperament, preferring change and new sensations, and are passionate about travel. They must reconcile the contradiction of their varying obsessions.

La Pêche
CHOCOLAT FELIX POTIN
JUIN
LE CANCER

ROMANTIC AND SENSITIVE

Cancer

Sensitive and romantic Cancerians seek a protective and reassuring cocoon where they can find kindness, attention and tenderness. As a result, the ardour shown by Aries can upset this sensitivity. However, they share the same attachment to family and the comforts of home with Taureans. They find the youthful Geminian spirit appealing. Two Cancerians together share the desire to form a stable couple and have lots of children, like in fairy tales. As for Leos, they are reassuring for Cancerians because have the same family values. Virgos' discretion and foresight are also considered assets for Cancerians, making them reliable partners. The tenderness, desire to please and romantic nature of Librans are a match for Cancerians' sentimental side. Scorpios are drawn to Cancerians' childlike charm and moonlike qualities. Cancerians and Sagittarians build their happiness on their sense of sharing and communication. Capricorns allow Cancerians to express their feelings without being judged. Aquarians are very independent and can tire of attention-seeking Cancerians. Cancerians and Pisceans lose themselves in the limbo of their powerful imagination. They are each drawn to their respective romantic side and each takes care of the other.

JUIN
Série 366 Nr. 6

A 'MOTHERING' COLLEAGUE

Cancer

When it comes to occupations, Cancerians often have a 'mothering' role. Compassionate and helpful, they like to listen, help and solve problems. Professions associated with family, social and paramedical services, human resources, early childhood and the elderly are appealing to them. Generally, all activities related to the world of childhood and the family suit their gentle and conciliatory personality, particularly as general and nursery nurses, social workers, early childhood teachers, paediatricians, teachers, childminders and healthcare assistants. They also have a spontaneous affinity with the animal world. Because they have strong ties to their roots, they enjoy working in the family business. They are also drawn to professions in the property and hotel businesses. They love to welcome guests to their guest house, holiday cottage or hotel. They have a keen interest in history and are passionate about professions related to the past or its preservation, such as antique dealer, historian, archaeologist and museum curator. Since they also like to pass on their knowledge, teaching suits them perfectly. Moreover, they prefer occupations where they deal with the public, given that the moon is associated with crowds. They are attracted to food shops and restaurants, and trades involving the sea and fishing. Finally, their artistic sensibility draws them to creative professions, such as illustrator or photographer, which rely on their imagination and manual skills.

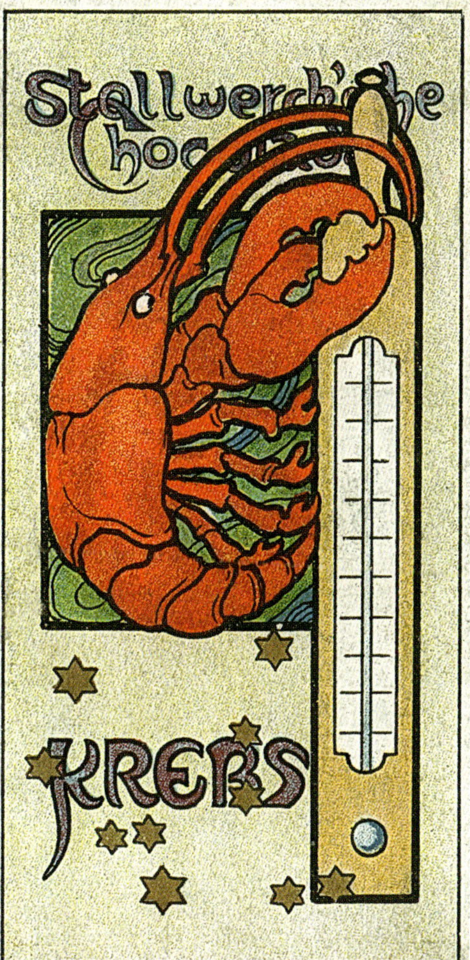
KREBS

THE LERNAEAN HYDRA

Cancer

The goddess Hera raised a monstrous nine-headed snake that made its lair near the Amymone spring and the Lerne marshes and terrorized the region. It was known as the Lernaean Hydra. The monster's heads, one of which was immortal, grew back when cut off. One of the twelve labours with which Heracles was tasked was to slay this beast. The hydra appeared to him aided by a giant crab (or crayfish) sent by Hera to distract the hero's attention. However, despite having his heel pinched tightly by the crab, Heracles managed to crush it underfoot. In spite of the intense pain he felt in his foot, he succeeded in trapping the hydra's heads under rocks and brought it down. Zeus, the chief of gods, then created the constellation of Cancer to immortalize the crustacean, a symbol of the protective world of people born under this sign. This animal prefers to bury itself in mud, close to its own kind, protected by its carapace. The myth of the hydra also shows the crab, or crayfish – representing the personality of Cancer – as being very tenacious and never giving up. Cancerians, like the hydra that lives in the depths of the marsh, retrieve ancestral and family memories from deep within in order to purge them. And the bodily pain of the pinch is a reminder that Cancerians must sometimes be brought back to reality, because they tend to live in their own imaginary world. The moon, the symbol of Cancer, represents fertility, femininity and sensitivity.

LES DOUZE TRAVAUX D'HERCULE - I.
2. - L'hydre de Lerne.
EXTRAIT DE VIANDE DE LA CIE LIEBIG

REMBRANDT, BETWEEN SHADOW AND LIGHT

Cancer

Rembrandt Harmenszoon van Rijn was born on 15 July 1606 in Leiden and died on 4 October 1669 in Amsterdam. Typically referred to as Rembrandt, he is considered one of the greats in the history of Western painting and the most important Dutch painter of the seventeenth century. He lived at a time known as the Dutch Golden Age, a period when the political, cultural, scientific and commercial influence of the Netherlands was at its height. His immense body of work consists of approximately 600 paintings, 300 etchings and 2,000 drawings. One of the particular features of his art was the technique of subtly modulating the effect of light against a dark background, creating contrasts to make his depictions of characters or objects stand out beautifully. All the Cancerian traits are to be found in his scenes of daily life, paintings of his family, portraits and self-portraits. His birth chart shows that the artist expressed his tormented emotions in his art, multiplied tenfold by his rising sign and the moon in Scorpio. His chiaroscuro technique perfectly reflects the mysterious side of this sign, which always fluctuates between shadow and light. Saturn in Capricorn can explain the personality of this solitary and often misunderstood man, who lived out his life in a plain and frugal manner. Rembrandt dedicated his entire life to his art.

REMBRANDT
Portrait of an Old Lady.

LEO, A MAJESTIC KING

Summer sign

Leo, the constellation of the lion, is the sign of people born between 23 July and 22 August. Leo has fire as its element and is ruled by the sun. Its lucky day is Sunday and its lucky number is 5. It has diamond as its stone, yellow as its colour and gold as its metal. Lilies are the favourite flowers of this sign. Its symbol depicts a lion's head that extends to a mane or tail. Leo is a sign of vitality and strength that gives a strong impression of power. Leos exude enjoyment of life. Ambitious and proud, they are radiant with the nobility they embody. Their independent nature makes them stand out and be noticed. Driven by the desire for power, they like to lead, unite and motivate the troops. They are generous, loving and paternalistic, and their charm, magnetism and warmth give them great appeal. They seek luxury, beauty and anything shiny. They are confident and prefer to think they are right. Though prone to anger, they are not resentful. They are upright and honest. They use their tremendous energy in the service of a company or a cause for the sake of posterity. They are traditionalists and conservative. They find it hard to question themselves. There are two types of Leos. The first are combative, materialistic and realistic, aiming for success and expansion. The second make honourable heroes and are endowed with spiritual and humanistic greatness. They are artists in search of beauty, idealists guided by their inner light and not by material success. Many of the great patrons of the arts are Leos.

La Distribution des Prix

A SUPERB AND GENEROUS BEING

Leo

Leos love nobly, genuinely and generously. They are also very keen on aesthetics. They have magnetism and natural class. Aries and Leos complement each other and shine together. They are two energetic temperaments that stimulate each other. Taureans and Leos share the same need for genuineness and both seek steady love. Leos are drawn to Geminians' chamaleonic nature and intellect. They provide reassurance for Cancer because both signs have great regard for family values. Two Leos together share a taste for luxury, beauty and the arts. They are very confident and proud of their success. Virgos' great intelligence wins over Leos, who are proud to appear with such cultivated and erudite partners. Leos are charmed by the elegance and innate class of Librans. Generous Leos rule supreme over their household. Leos and Scorpios are connected by their tremendous magnetism and aura. Their feelings are intense and passionate. Drawn to the loyalty and generosity of Leos, Sagittarians allow themselves to be conquered by their magnetism and overconfidence. Ambitious Capricorns and success-seeking Leos share common goals. On the other hand, Leos' paternalism and authority may offend the sensibility of Aquarians, leading them to feel trapped. Because they are valued and supported by Pisceans, Leos strive to preserve their union.

JUILLET
Serie 366 Nr.

A BRILLIANT BOSS

Leo

Leos need to feel appreciated and recognized. No matter what they do, they want to be the best. They are gifted with a great capacity for work and a passion for organizing, creating and being in charge. Because they combine flexibility with determination and generosity with discipline, they know how to encourage and energize their staff and reassure partners. Their initiatives always favour the group. Being very positive, they do not envisage failure, and everything they undertake has to succeed. Scrupulous, exacting and ambitious, they accomplish their goals through cunning schemes and self-control. As a result, they rise to important positions, such as those of manager, politician and senior civil servant. They also make excellent ambassadors. Leos often set up their own companies. The world of business, sales, marketing and advertising holds no secrets for them. They are talented sales representatives and masterfully lead negotiations. They appreciate money and will do anything to earn it. They make excellent financiers. What is more, they also prefer professions involving the public and representation: they want to shine and be admired. They are drawn to the world of creativity, which is why they work in professions dealing with luxury, art and fashion, such as jeweller, model, interior designer and art director. Leos are also partial to the world of show business, entertainment and cinema, and they can be found in the fields of film-making, stage directing and conducting.

CHICORÉE AU DERNIER TAMBOUR
CASIEZ & BOURGEOIS
à Cambrai
LE LION

THE NEMEAN LION

Leo

The first of the labours with which Heracles was tasked was to kill a fearsome beast. In the forest of Nemea, in Argolis, there lived a lion of extraordinary strength that was devouring all the livestock in the region. The beast was the son of Selene, the goddess of the moon, and was reputed to be invincible, protected by a skin that was impenetrable to arrows. After several unsuccessful attempts armed with a club, the hero only succeeded in stunning it. Realizing then that he could only defeat it by using his courage, determination and strength, he gripped the lion with both hands and gradually strangled it. After his victory, he clothed himself in the lion's skin as armour and wore its head as a helmet. In this myth, Heracles is the embodiment of Leo's feeling of superiority and invincibility. By saving the inhabitants of the area from the beast that terrorized them, he also showed the generosity, social awareness and altruism that characterize this sign. Leo is a symbol of power and people born under this sign are potent fighters endowed with great confidence. They never hesitate to cause confrontation in order to surmount difficulties. They are often presented as very committed defenders, who know how to overcome their own fears and become a hero admired by all.

LES DOUZE TRAVAUX D'HERCULE - I.
1. - Le lion de Némée.
EXTRAIT DE VIANDE DE LA CIE LIEBIG

NAPOLEON THE CONQUEROR

Leo

Napoleon Bonaparte was born on 15 August 1769 in Ajaccio and died on 5 May 1821 on the island of Saint Helena. He left Corsica at the age of ten to complete his military education on the French mainland. He was appointed General-in-Chief of the French Army of Italy in 1796, and on 9 March of that year, he married Joséphine de Beauharnais, with whom he was infatuated. Venus in Cancer in his birth chart shows that he hoped to start a family and have children. The Pluto opposition, which unleashed his passion and jealousy, may explain his repudiation of his wife after she was unable to bear him an heir. His quest for power drove him to greater things. The Coup of 18 Brumaire led to his appointment as first consul, before he was crowned Emperor Napoleon I on 2 December 1804. He modernized all French public institutions by creating the Civil Code, the Legion of Honour and the secondary education system, and reforming justice, finance and administration. His Scorpio ascendant made him very exacting, with a keen sense of perfection and a calculating, cold and fixated mind. By drawing on his endless supply of energy (Mars trine Uranus), he became the warmongering emperor and a masterful strategist. He was a veritable warlord who set out to conquer Europe, and his victories came in succession, such as at Austerlitz (1805), Jena (1806) and Wagram (1809), among others... But his costly campaigns also ended in defeat, such as the Invasion of Russia (1812) and the Battle of Waterloo (1815).

CHICORÉE
A LA
BERGÈRE
ÉMILE
BONZEL
HAUBOURDIN (Nord)
(80) NAPOLEON Ier

VIRGO, THE DISCREET ORGANIZER

Summer sign

Virgo, the constellation of the virgin, is the sign of people born between 23 August and 22 September. Virgo has earth as its element and is ruled by the planet Mercury. Its lucky day is Wednesday and its lucky number is six. It has amethyst as its stone, purple as its colour and platinum as its metal. Violets are the favourite flowers of this sign. Its symbol depicts a series of arches, indicating secrecy and brooding. It ends by turning in on itself, reinforcing the idea of introversion. This sign of precision and care represents work and thought. Virgos are reserved and rational, and show discernment and prudence. They make excellent, active and meticulous merchants. They are acutely perfectionist, with very keen intelligence and intense brain activity. Conscientious and hard-working Virgos have a taste for order, sometimes obsessively so. Their sense of analysis and perfection makes them hesitant when having to choose, out of fear of making mistakes. They have an acutely critical mind. Virgos are dedicated and like to be of service. Nevertheless, their attention to detail prevents them from seeing the forest for the trees. They often specialize in a certain field. There are two types of Virgos. The first are cerebral, reserved, shy, serious, rational and meticulous. They are hesitant and lack confidence. They are also very thrifty. The second are messy and unconventional, their cerebral side giving way to instinct , creativity, rebelliousness and originality.

AOÛT
LA VIERGE
♍
Les Bains de Mer

A SENSITIVE AND MODEST SIGN

Virgo

Virgos are affectionate and discreet, sensitive and modest. Their critical mind makes them very choosy when it comes to love. Their foresight and prudence calm fiery Aries. The Virgo-Taurus couple is ideal because the former seduces the latter very gently. Virgos also appreciate Geminians for their youthful nature, but the instability of this sign makes them feel insecure. In the Cancer-Virgo couple, the former takes care of the education of the children and managing the home, while the latter takes care of the day-to-day routine. Virgos bring Leos common sense and organizational skills, while Leos contribute in return with their ambition and passions. Two Virgos together have a sense of perfection. Extroverted Librans express their feelings to Virgos, who find it difficult to show what they feel and are surprised at their partners' need to socialize. Scorpios open the doors of an unexpected universe to Virgos, who are drawn to their differences. Sagittarians, who take life as it comes, with ease and optimism, find it difficult to understand Virgos' doubts and anxiety, and tendency to split hairs. Capricorns and Virgos, both earth signs, support each other and are unfailingly devoted to each other. Aquarians, however, can barely stand the Virgos' obsession with order and precision. Finally, Pisceans are brought back to reality by Virgos, although the latter are not very reassured by the formers' passionate nature.

ZODIAQUE. LA VIERGE ET LA BALANCE.

METICULOUS AND RESERVED

Virgo

The sign of Virgo represents daily work, health and cleanliness. Virgos are dedicated and often choose a profession in the medical or paramedical fields, such as laboratory technician, doctor, nurse, researcher, pharmacist, veterinarian, osteopath or naturopath. Their taste for numbers, filing and organization also lead them into careers as accountants, analysts, clerks, booksellers, librarians and archivists. These meticulous perfectionists like occupations involving precision and research, such as that of watchmaker, optician and locksmith. They also have a sense of duty, a reputation for being humble and virtuous, even shy, but very hard-working. Virgos tend to rise slowly to positions of responsibility, as many among them have an inferiority complex and do not dare to assert themselves. Worriers by nature, they iron out all the details and check everything thoroughly because they fear being criticized. They have an analytical mind and are appreciated for their intellectual qualities. Virgos want to be perfect and, above all, need to feel useful. Because their sign is ruled by Mercury, they are interested in everything that concerns writing, studies and communication. They work methodically and apply themselves, which is why Virgos are considered the worker bees of the zodiac. Tedious tasks do not frighten Virgos; on the contrary, they are stimulated by them as soon as everything is in order. Even when they succeed professionally, Virgos always remain very modest.

Août
Les Chaleurs.
La Vierge
Huntley & Palmers
Biscuits
Reading & London

DEMETER
Virgo

The incomparably beautiful Persephone was born out of the union between Demeter and her brother Zeus. Her father had been planning to marry her to Hades, the god of the underworld, and was forced to set a trap in order to release her from her mother's protection. One day, as the young girl was about to pick a beautiful narcissus, the ground opened beneath her and she fell into the underworld. Demeter, the goddess of harvest and seasons, was outraged and abandoned her duties, threatening mankind with starvation. In order to appease his sister's anger, Zeus asked Hades to send their daughter back to him. But the god of the underworld did not agree. He made his wife eat the seeds of a pomegranate so that she would forever be united with him. However, a solution was found to satisfy everybody. Persephone would spend part of the year with Demeter and the rest with Hades. Spring, summer and autumn are joyful seasons because Persephone is happily by her mother's side. Then comes dark and cold winter, the season when Persephone must return to the underworld. This myth is analogous to the symbolism of Virgo, a sign of devotion and service to the cycles of daily life, work and rest, which are just like those of sowing and harvesting. Virgos are very far-sighted and are afraid to be caught short, but they are never impervious to having their best-laid plans go awry. This sign represents fertility and human and social achievement through work.

CHOCOLAT
MEURISSE
ANVERS
Série 21 N° 2
MYTHOLOGIE. - Déméter de Cnide

GOETHE, THE DISCIPLINE OF A VIRGO

Virgo

Johann Wolfgang von Goethe was born in Frankfurt am Main on 28 August 1749 and died in Weimar on 22 March 1832. 'There's a real man!' is what Napoleon said of this prolific poet, novelist and playwright who dominated the German literary scene for more than fifty years. But he was also a scientist and an excellent administrator. As an exemplary Virgo, he was passionate about the natural sciences and interested in the laws of nature and the secrets it held. Among other works, he is credited with writing the essay *The Metamorphosis of Plants*, which was published in 1790. But his greatest achievement is *Faust*. The writing of this tragedy occupied him for sixty years. His sun sign of Virgo and the presence of Saturn near the ascendant brought him a sense of perfection, precision, discipline and critical thinking. Moreover, his ascendant and Pluto in Scorpio explain the tragic and dark side of his character Faust, who was tempted by a pact with the Devil. Goethe took an interest in astrology in 1811, under the influence of one of his mother's friends, who also aroused his curiosity for mysticism, occultism and alchemy. As he explained, 'Astrology is not synonymous with fatalism. It allows us to make out the structure of a human being or a group, and where our structure is fixed, we are nevertheless free to develop the contents of such a structure. The games of life are a fact, but in a given game, everyone can play a different part.'

LA JOUVENCE DE L'ABBÉ SOURY

LA JOUVENCE DE L'ABBÉ SOURY

LA JOUVENCE DE L'ABBÉ SOURY

(*Johann Wolfgang*). *Le plus grand poète de l'Allemagne. Né à Francfort en 1749, mort à Weimar en 1832.*

LA JOUVENCE DE L'ABBÉ SOURY

LIBRA, THE ANGEL OF LOVE

Autumn sign

Libra, the constellation of the scales, is the sign of people born between 23 September and 22 October. Libra has air as its element and is ruled by the planet Venus. Its lucky day is Friday and its lucky number is seven. It has jade as its stone, green as its colour and cobalt as its metal. Gladioli are the favourite flowers of this sign. Its symbol consists of two horizontal lines, with a semicircle inserted into the upper line representing the Egyptian hieroglyphic for balance. Individuals born under the sign of Libra tend to weigh and measure. They seek justice and balance, like the instrument that symbolizes them. They are idealists on a quest for peace and harmony, eschewing conflict. Fair and conciliatory, Librans take their time when choosing, systematically weighing the pros and cons. They are slow to make up their mind and have trouble deciding. They are lovers of art and aesthetics, appreciating beauty in all its forms. They have an exceptional talent for relationships because they favour sharing within a group. They flourish in a serene environment. There are two types of Librans. The first are extroverted and exude warmth. They love contact, exchange and communication, and they thrive by being friendly to everybody. Their approachable, open, generous and sociable nature gives them great appeal. The second type, however, are introverted and anxious, retreating out of fear of being hurt by the outside world. They are reserved, calm and quiet.

Septembre
LA BALANCE
La Chasse

AN INNATE CHARMER

Libra

Librans' innate charm makes them appealing. Libra is the sign of love and people born under this sign are looking for their soul mate. Being faithful and sensitive, their romantic relationships tend to be profound. Aries are disarmed by Librans' gentle charm. They share Taureans' powerful sensuality and Geminians' optimism and sociability. They will seek to balance fluctuating Cancerian moods with gestures of tenderness and words that express their love. Leos fall titillated under the spell of Libran elegance and natural generosity. However, Librans are likely to find Virgos disruptive. Two Librans together, on the other hand, bathe in the glow of shared happiness. Sensual Scorpios allow themselves to be charmed by the Librans' sensitivity but may find their intransigence hurtful. Sagittarians are moved by their open-mindedness, tolerance and refinement. In return, Librans love their optimistic view of the world. Capricorns help Librans to make decisions, to assert themselves and to find balance. There is obvious compatibility between Aquarians and Librans, both air signs. Pisceans and Librans both have strong demands for affection. Librans make ideal partners for Pisceans, even if the latter sometimes lack a sense of reality.

SEPTEMBRE.
OCTOBRE.
VII
VIII
Liebig
LA BALANCE.
LE SCORPION.
VÉRITABLE
EXTRAIT
DE VIANDE LIEBIG.
Le soleil entre dans ce signe vers le
23 Septembre.
Fable: Thémis régna en Thessalie
avec tant de sagesse et d'équité
qu'on en fit la déesse de la justice.
Les signes
du Zodiaque.
Le soleil entre dans ce signe vers le
23 Octobre.
Fable: Orion osa défier Diane
qui, pour le punir, le fit piquer
par un scorpion.
Voir au verso.

A PROFESSIONAL TIGHTROPE WALKER

Libra

Librans possess great interpersonal qualities and a great sense of contact. They value association, partnerships and community life. They like to harmonize, balance, reconcile, measure and select. They make ideal partners and collaborators. Librans work very conscientiously and consistently. They are drawn to the fields of human resources, commerce, communications, public relations, journalism and tourism. However, it takes them a long time to find their true calling. They can therefore change jobs several times in the course of their career. They also make excellent managers who know how to value the work of their staff by creating an atmosphere of trust and tranquillity. Librans are very friendly and diplomatic, and they have a sense of acceptance and good listening skills. They like to work in a relaxed atmosphere or a place where they feel comfortable. Libra represents the middle ground. Librans will therefore be reluctant to take sides in the event of conflict. Artistic professions, such as fashion designer, stylist, model, beautician, make-up artist and hairdresser, are perfectly suited to them. They can also work as decorators, art dealers and interior designers. Being innate defenders, they are drawn to the professions of justice and mediation, including those of lawyer, judge, marriage counsellor and social worker.

SEPTEMBRE
La Chasse.
Les Balances
HUNTLEY & PALMERS
BISCUITS
Reading & London

PSYCHE

Libra

Psyche was the daughter of a king. She was so beautiful that no one dared to approach her. Aphrodite, the goddess of love, was so resentful of her that she asked her son Eros to make Psyche fall in love with a hideous creature. However, as he was on his way to accomplish his mission, Eros fell under the spell of her beauty and took her away with him to a beautiful palace and fulfilled all his beloved's desires, on the condition that the young girl should never try to look at him. Alas, one night when she was unable to resist any longer, she lit a candle and a drop of wax fell on her lover's face. She was able to behold his divine beauty, but she had betrayed their pact. Eros immediately vanished, and so did his palace. When Aphrodite discovered that her son was having an affair with her rival, she condemned her to perform a large number of difficult and humiliating tasks. Psyche overcame them with the invaluable assistance of her lover's allies. Eros then begged Zeus to make her immortal, a wish he granted. Psyche became a goddess and then married Eros. The association between this myth and this sign is obvious. A Libran, a refined and charming lover of beauty, seeks love with a capital L. He must look beyond appearances and not rely solely on outward beauty. It is also the sign of justice, because Psyche was punished for her disobedience by undergoing a series of trials. It therefore shows that Librans seek balance in all areas of their existence.

AMORE E PSICHE

GANDHI, THE MESSENGER OF TOLERANCE

Libra

Mohandas Karamchand Ghandi was born on 2 October 1869 in Porbandar, in the Indian state of Gujarat, and was assassinated in Delhi on 30 January 1948. He was born into an affluent family and raised with Hindu values, but he showed interest in other religions. When he was fourteen, his parents married him off to Kasturba, who remained his wife until his death. Ghandi studied in London to become a lawyer. He later moved to South Africa in 1893, where he won his first victories against racial injustice in that country. He returned to India in 1915. Uranus, which symbolizes freedom, revolution and transformation, has an important place in his birth chart. Ghandi became a great political and spiritual leader and fought for his country's independence by advocating non-violence. The position of the sun in his chart and his Libra ascendant confirm his desire for harmony, tolerance and his ideal of justice, earning him his honorific title *Mahatma*, Sanskrit for 'great-souled', and also *Bapu*, 'father'. Moreover the moon in Leo reveals his fame. He was very religious and lived modestly in an ashram. He fasted rigorously to purify himself, but also in protest against the rampant violence in India. He spent his entire life seeking the truth, developing all the qualities associated with Saturn, including wisdom, patience, simplicity and austerity, together with the idealism and optimism resulting from its presence in Sagittarius.

INDES ANGLAISES _ Le Mahatma Gandhi

SCORPIO, SECRET AND MYSTERIOUS

Autumn sign

Scorpio, the constellation of the scorpion, is the sign of people born between 23 October and 22 November. Scorpio has water as its element and is ruled by the planet Pluto. Its lucky day is Tuesday and its number is eight. It has garnet as its stone, dark red as its colour and iron as its metal. Anthuriums are the favourite flowers of this sign. Its symbol is an M ending in an arrow or a sting. Scorpios have a formidable psyche. Engrossed by the invisible world, they have an innate taste for probing into how and why things happen. They are highly perceptive, enigmatic and elusive. They have a rational, intelligent and critical mind. Their opinion is very clear-cut; it is either love or hate. They are also psychic. They act with vehemence, and the same effort can go into building up or undermining themselves. They are resolute and independent, except with their emotions, where they become possessive and jealous, and they fall passionately in love. Yet they are very sensitive and hide their emotions, unwilling to expose themselves. Scorpios are brave, tenacious and zealous. They inspire awe and their piercing gaze is alluring. But they can hold a grudge. There are two types of Scorpios. The first are orderly, stable, methodical, clear and conventional. They are extremely discreet, so it is difficult to know what they are thinking. The second are rebellious, verging on anarchic. They are profligate and uncontrollably indulgent. They are superstitious and incredibly intuitive.

OCTOBRE
LE SCORPION
ECOLE
TOTO
La Rentrée des Classes

STORMY PASSIONS

Scorpio

Scorpios find love under stormy skies. Their impulses sometimes overwhelm them and their relationships are often passionate. Aries and Scorpios both have powerful instincts and each wants to be in control. Scorpios often use authoritarian tactics to impose their ideas on Taureans, who will not give way. While they can find the Geminian lightness of spirit appealing, they can also just as easily find it exasperating. When it comes to Cancerians, Scorpios drown in a sea of passions that are filled with crises and making up. Scorpios and Leos are connected by their magnetism and powerful aura. Scorpios drive Virgos to be bold. In return, Virgos provide them with calm. Scorpios are unable to resist Libran charm. The taste for mystery and experimentation brings two Scorpios together, each of whom keeps little secrets. Their exclusive and possessive nature can scare away freedom and space-loving Sagittarians. But they manage to overcome Capricorns' reserve by leading them into an unexpected waltz of fantasy that leaves them bewildered. The visionary side of Aquarians and Scorpios brings them together, but their relationship is often of a cerebral nature, while Scorpios are looking for sensuality. Scorpios and Pisceans come to a meeting of souls. Pisceans fall under the mysterious and bewitching spell of their Scorpio partners.

OKTOBRE
Serie 366 Nr. 10

THE KING OF DETECTIVES

Scorpio

Because they like to unravel mysteries, Scorpios are drawn to investigative occupations. As they are endowed with deep intelligence, they analyse, peel away and dissect. They also make highly successful interrogators, leaving nothing to chance. They use their powers of deduction and sense of observation in their work. Scorpios like to reveal the psychological and physical workings in humans. This is why they are often found in the medical professions as psychiatrists, psychologists, forensic pathologists, surgeons and gynaecologists. But they also shine in law enforcement, in roles such as detective and forensic scientist, and in the security industry. Scorpios also make use of their extraordinary intuition in areas related to clairvoyance, mediumship, mesmerism and astrology. Their incredible intuition allows them to excel in the world of finance and buying and selling property. Authoritative and independent Scorpios like to be in charge. They are endowed with a powerful energy, an unparalleled fighting spirit, determination, courage, and perseverance beyond compare. They are impassioned people who give their all for their work. They are very ambitious and are able to show great detachment in order to achieve their goals. No obstacle is too great for these relentless workers and no situation escapes their attention; they are in total control. They are at their best in complicated, stressful and even extreme situations. Scorpios seek power, money and social standing.

OCTOBRE
9 K.
Les Vendanges.
HUNTLEY & PALMERS
BISCUITS
Reading & London
Le Scorpion

ORION
Scorpio

Orion, a giant renowned for his beauty and hunting skills, fell in love with Merope, the daughter of King Oenopion. However, in the course of a drunken feast, he wounded his beloved's father with a few unfortunate words. Seeking vengeance, the king appealed to Dionysus, who blinded Orion, leaving him to wander in the darkness. The unfortunate man consulted an oracle, who advised him to walk to the place where the sun rose in order to regain his sight. When he arrived at his destination, he found that he had received a sense of perception and intuition that no mortal possessed. He later went to serve the goddess Artemis and met Eos, the goddess of the dawn and symbol of birth and rebirth, with whom he fell in love. However, the jealous Artemis brought a fearsome scorpion out of the earth to kill Orion. To show her gratitude to the creature, she created the constellation of Scorpio. She did the same with Orion, placing him at the opposite end of the sky so that they would never meet again. The scorpion of the myth is a good analogy for the sign of Scorpio and its constant evolution and transformation. It symbolizes destruction and reconstruction, and perpetual rebirth. As for Orion, despite his debauched life, he ended up high in the sky, in the constellation that bears his name. Like the creature of myth, Scorpios lie in the shadows and wait for their prey. They keep their secrecy and mystery and have the gift of finding the flaws in each individual.

CONSTELLATION.
ORION.
Projected by right Ascension and Declination.
Corrected to the beginning of the Year 1808.
PLATE 1
Right Ascension in Time
VI Hours
LEPUS
Right Ascension in Degrees
North Polar Distance
South Declination
North Declination
AEQUINOCTIALIS
Double
Clust.
Nebulae

MARIE-ANTOINETTE THE INDEPENDENT

Scorpio

Marie-Antoinette de Lorraine-Habsbourg was born on 2 November 1755 in Vienna, Austria, and died by the guillotine on 16 October 1793 in Paris. She was the sister of Holy Roman Emperors Joseph II and Leopold II, and she held the titles of archduchess of Austria, imperial princess and royal princess of Hungary and Bohemia. However, it was as the wife of King Louis XVI that she gained most fame. Her beauty and allure, from the presence of the sun and Venus in Scorpio, gave the queen of France a bewitching charm. She was sensitive to beauty and art, thanks to the moon in Libra, and she was very elegant. She loved amusement, parties and a life of leisure, and she entertained lavishly. Being very independent, she spent a lot of time in the hamlet she had built in the park of the palace of Versailles, where she introduced her children and guests to the charms of country life. Uranus rules her birth chart, which explains the uncompromising and non conformist side of her that was so disliked. Because she refused to sacrifice her personal life for her duties as a queen and sought more freedom, she embodied the new aspirations of her time. Likewise, she was fiercely opposed to a constitutional monarchy. Marie-Antoinette appeared before the Revolutionary Court on 14 October 1793. Her trial, unlike that of her husband Louis XVI, was not a fair one. She was subsequently convicted of high treason and executed two days later.

Marie Antoinette

SAGITTARIUS, A KNIGHT IN SHINING ARMOUR

Autumn sign

Sagittarius, the constellation of the centaur, is the sign of people born between 23 November and 21 December. Sagittarius has fire as its element and is ruled by the planet Jupiter. Its lucky day is Thursday and its lucky number is nine. It has turquoise as its stone, orange as its colour and tin as its metal. Bird of Paradise is the favourite flower of this sign. Its symbol consists of an arrow pointing upwards, expressing the search for spirituality. A perpendicular line divides the arrow to indicate the duality between matter and spirit. Sagittarians need space and new horizons. They love other cultures and travelling, and show interest in religion, philosophy, foreign languages and higher education. They are generally lucky. They are ardent, enthusiastic and particularly epicurean. They also like sport and the open air. Their generosity leads them to espouse worthy political or humanitarian causes. There are three types of Sagittarians. Marked by Jupiter, the first are conventional, optimistic and devoted to public affairs in search of honour and prestige. Their taste for power drives them to be leaders. The second are rebellious, like the heroes you find in Westerns. Spirited and energetic, they rebel against convention and fight against taboos and prejudices. They make explorers, adventurers, sportspeople and fighters. The last are inward-looking philosophers. They are explorers of the mind on a quest for spirituality.

NOVEMBRE
LE SAGITTAIRE
Les Boules de Neige

AN IDEALIST WITH PLENTY OF LOVE TO GIVE

Sagittarius

Sagittarians are energetic and straightforward, with a focus on results. They idealize and seek relationships with different cultures. Their generosity is appealing to Aries. They share their interest in sensual and epicurean pleasures with Taureans. When paired with Geminians, they are capable of setting off on a spontaneous adventure; while with Cancerians, their happiness is founded on the family, although their partners would like them to spend more time at home. The couple formed by Leo and Sagittarius brings fireworks. Sagittarians make every effort to understand and reassure Virgos. In return, Virgos rein in their partners' impulses. Sagittarians appreciate Libran tolerance and refinement. They bring enjoyment of life and optimism to Scorpios, giving them a new outlook on things. Two Sagittarians together have a passion for travel and adventure, and each idealizes the other. They share their excellent strength of character with Capricorns, allowing them to overcome obstacles and cope with difficulties. The relationship between Sagittarians and Aquarians is based on mutual trust and a common idealism. Because both their signs are idealistic and generous, Pisceans and Sagittarians are forever united by their passion for humanitarianism and spirituality.

Chaussures Raoul
1, Boulevard Saint-Denis
LE SAGITTAIRE

PATERNALISTIC RIGHTER OF WRONGS

Sagittarius

Enterprising Sagittarians demonstrate great optimism and a strong will to succeed. They refuse to sit still in their jobs. They seek contact and exchange, and they also have a need to play a social role and assert themselves within a group. They like to connect, coordinate, organize and make the rules. Because they are concerned about legality, they often find careers in justice-related professions. They bring their drive, spirit and generosity to the workplace. They appreciate teamwork and enjoy sharing their knowledge and experience. Endowed with plenty of common sense, they have a broad and clear vision of any situation, which allows them to perfectly control their actions. They are skilful with words and know how to convince. Because of their paternalistic side, they can be bossy at times. And while they admire their superiors, they can also be quite unruly. They can be found in education, in such roles as teachers of higher education and specialist teachers. They also go into professions in the tourism industry, as travel agents and as interpreters and guides; and in any international roles, including journalists, special correspondents, doctors on humanitarian missions, ambassadors and politicians. On the spiritual side, they can be priests and theologians, but also philosophers. As opportunists, they always manage to find the right people in the right place to help them advance.

Stollwerck'sche Chocolade

Schütze

THE CENTAURS

Sagittarius

Centaurs are mythological creatures that are part man and part horse. They were considered supernatural beings of the mountains and forests that represented both light and darkness. Pholos was an exception among the centaurs. He was friendly, wise and kind. He welcomed Heracles when he came to hunt the Erymanthian boar. To celebrate the hero's arrival, Pholos prepared a feast with which he served a delicious wine given to him by Dionysus for this special occasion. However, the other centaurs were drawn by the smell of this fragrant drink and came uninvited to his table. They attacked Heracles, who repelled them with arrows soaked in the venom of the Lernaean hydra. Alas, one of them mortally wounded Pholos. Heracles was saddened by the death of his host and arranged a sumptuous funeral for him. He also named a mountain in his honour, Mount Pholoe. This myth characterizes Sagittarians. They are instinctive and, like Pholos who enjoyed life's pleasures, they are epicurean. They are depicted as a centaur aiming his arrow at the sky, symbolizing the will of humans to choose their own destiny by endeavouring to hit the target. It points the way to evolution and to transforming desires in order to achieve a spiritual or intellectual aspiration.

Voir au verso.

BEETHOVEN, A REBELLIOUS LIBERTARIAN

Sagittarius

Ludwig van Beethoven was born in Bonn, Germany, on 16 December 1770 and died in Vienna on 26 March 1827. He was a composer and pianist and his works marked the transition to Romantic music. His work of expanding genres set the scene for the musical evolution of the nineteenth century. With Scorpio as his rising sign, Beethoven was subjected to a series of trials: the death of four of his seven brothers and sisters; the death of his mother, to whom he was very close; and his deafness, which worsened until it became total. Saturn in the house that rules career on his birth chart, shows that he was forced into self-isolation for fear that the truth would be known. He was labelled a misanthropist and he suffered greatly as a result. Mars in Gemini may symbolize his ear and hearing problems. But far from giving in to despair, this Sagittarius placed great faith in his art, and his symphonies still hold an important place in the history of music today. The best-known work, his *Ninth Symphony*, corresponds to the house of Sagittarius in astrology. With Neptune in the house that rules career, one might suggest that his music was divinely inspired. Uranus in Taurus, however, made him rebellious and independent. Beethoven was very popular with women and he dedicated some of his masterpieces to them, such as *Für Elise* and *Moonlight Sonata*. His total deafness allowed him to exploit all his creative genius and experience his inner dreams.

COMPOSITEURS CÉLÈBRES.
LOUIS BEETHOVEN,
Né le 16 Décembre 1770 à Bonn
(Allemagne).
Mort le 27 Mars 1827 à Vienne.
„FIDELIO." „SONATES."
„SYMPHONIES." „MESSE SOLENNELLE."
VÉRITABLE EXTRAIT DE VIANDE LIEBIG.
VOIR AU VERSO.

CAPRICORN, AN ENLIGHTENED HERMIT

Winter sign

Capricorn, the constellation of the goat, is the sign of people born between 22 December and 20 January. Capricorn has earth as its element and is ruled by the planet Saturn. Its lucky day is Saturday and its lucky number is seven. It has onyx as its stone, brown as its colour and lead as its metal. Primroses are the favourite flowers of this sign. Its symbol represents withdrawing into oneself to form a loop. Capricorns love solitude, which they need in order to unwind and recover their strength. Prudent and steadfast, Capricorns have a sense of duty. Their sign is one of discipline, tenacity and power. They are introverted, move cautiously and take an interest in difficult problems that require effort to solve. Nothing distracts them from their purpose and endeavours. They face life one step at a time, thus rising slowly and in stages. Loyal friends and faithful lovers, they are very serious and cannot bear betrayal. Capricorns are as demanding of others as they are of themselves and are very reliable friends. They are materialistic and thrifty, and very far-sighted. Capricorn is also a sign of maturity and longevity. There are two types of Capricorns. The first are ambitious, domineering and stubborn. By doggedly keeping to their path, they often have very successful careers, reaching positions of great responsibility. The second type are detached from their material circumstances and devote themselves to a noble or spiritual cause.

Noël
Décembre
LE CAPRICORNE

FIRE UNDER THE ICE

Capricorn

People born under the sign of Capricorn find it difficult to express their feelings, which are nevertheless deep and sincere. Commitment and dedication are very important to them. Their sensible, serious and quiet nature calms the ardours of Aries. When paired with Taurus, they very quickly seek out a cosy little nest to make their own. With lively and curious Geminians, conventional and ambitious Capricorns develop good intellectual relations. Cancerians appreciate the security and sense of conventionality their Capricorn partners bring. Capricorns yield their place in the spotlight to Leos. They are calm and stable with Virgos, forming a couple with their feet planted firmly on the ground. They grant Librans a great deal of freedom in order to make their relationship work. However, they allow themselves to be influenced by Scorpios for their greater happiness. They must adapt to Sagittarians' steady pace, which takes them out of their comfort zone. Two Capricorns appreciate each other for their common values of stability and trust. However, they have a difficult time coping with Aquarians, whom they find too original and eccentric. As for Pisceans, they feel protected and fulfilled by a reliable, stable and disciplined Capricorn partner.

DEZEMBER
Serie 366 Nr. 12

AMBITIOUS BUT FAIR

Capricorn

Capricorns naturally look for occupations that require patience, discipline and perseverance. Being very ambitious, they make it a point to achieve material success. Their sense of organization and perfection, and their great capacity for concentration often lead them into scientific careers in the fields of aeronautics, engineering and research. They prefer work involving minute detail. In the medical field, they are often found as surgeons. Their excellent memory makes them enthusiastic about history-related professions. They are drawn to activities connected with heritage management, archaeology and exploring caves. As Capricorns feel more comfortable on their own, they like to be in control and delegate little. They are realistic and very objective. Their strong sense of discipline often leads them to embark on military or political careers. Their success often comes late, but it is lasting. As they find fulfilment in their work, they can devote all their time to it without ever veering off course. They are always reliable and their skills are in high demand. Their immense need for security means they rarely change direction. They make good managers who never allow their emotions to guide them. They remain objective and always act fairly.

DÉCEMBRE
l'Hiver.
Le Capricorne
HUNTLEY & PALMERS
BISCUITS
Reading & London

AMALTHEA
Capricorn

As soon as he was born, Zeus was hidden away in the mountains of Crete so that his father Cronus would not devour him as he had his other siblings. He was entrusted to Amalthea, a she-goat with the tail of a fish, who nourished the divine infant with her milk. When she died, the now adult Zeus adorned his shield with her skin. This fabulous defensive device, which was forged by Hephaestus, the god of Fire, enabled him to win many battles. Once, when Amalthea broke a horn, Zeus returned it to her with the promise that it would forever be filled with flowers and fruits. This is how the famous Horn of Plenty was created. Capricorn is an ambitious, power-hungry sign. Like the goat that lives on steep slopes, Capricorns use their perseverance to aim for the heights. Both are tireless climbers who ascend to the very top of the mountains, braving obstacles without looking back. And both rely only on themselves. Often detached and solitary, Capricorns tend to seek high ground. They rid themselves of everything superfluous and sometimes impose drastic living conditions in order to enable themselves to advance. Amalthea's fish tail symbolizes the spirituality of this sign. This myth illustrates the destiny of the Capricorn who, after reaching the heights of success, offers assistance to whoever asks.

JUPITER.
1.— La naissance de Jupiter.

PASTEUR, AN UNCOMPROMISING INVENTOR

Capricorn

Louis Pasteur was born in Dole on 27 December 1822 and died in Marnes-la-Coquette on 28 September 1895. He was a chemist and biologist and was renowned for his work in the life sciences, in fields such as hygiene, medicine, biology and agriculture. We have him to thank for the rabies vaccine, which he developed in 1885. He had previously demonstrated the existence of germs and studied fermentation. In 1865, he invented the pasteurization process that improved the preservation of food. He also made important discoveries in chemistry, particularly at the molecular level. He was elected a member of the Académie Française in 1881 and he became director of the institute that bears his name in 1887. His birth chart is exceptional. This tireless researcher had six planets in the sign of Capricorn in the house that rules study, communication and research. Thanks to the presence of Mercury and Uranus in this sign, his capacities of analysis, investigation and invention were enhanced. The moon in Gemini indicates great alertness and insatiable curiosity. His Libra rising sign may explain his simple, harmonious life, love of art and hidden talent for painting and drawing.

(Louis). *Grand savant français né à Dôle (Jura) en 1822, mort à Villeneuve-l'Etang en 1895.*

AQUARIUS, THE INSPIRED INNOVATOR

Winter sign

Aquarius, the constellation of the water bearer, is the sign of people born between 21 January and 18 February. Aquarius has air as its element and is ruled by the planet Uranus. Its lucky day is Saturday and its lucky number is three. It has rock crystal as its stone, dark blue as its colour and platinum as its metal. Orchids are the favourite flowers of this sign. Its symbol consists of two parallel wavy lines separated by an expanse of air. Aquarians are as fluid as a wind-swept ocean. Their experimental mind is focused on knowledge, research and their passion for new technologies. Free-thinking and progressive Aquarians challenge convention. Rather than contemplating their existence from the sidelines, they act. Their ambition is to work for future generations. They are intellectual, ingenious inventors and innovative visionaries who look to the future. They can sometimes have an idealistic view of life. Their motto is liberty, fraternity and equality. They are altruistic, detached and serene, with a sense of cooperation and solidarity. There are two types of Aquarians. The influence of Uranus makes the first revolutionary, adventurous and original. Fiercely independent, they shake up convention and go where few dare to tread. Progress and modernity fascinate this genius. The second cultivate their inner wisdom, detaching themselves from the material in order to achieve their ideals. Not worried about daily constraints, they often live as if they were on another planet.

CHOCOLAT FÉLIX POTIN
JANVIER
LE VERSEAU
Les Etrennes

AN ALTRUISTIC LOVER

Aquarius

Aquarians seek fraternal love, which is sometimes confused with friendship. Their idea of love is broad, unconventional and altruistic. This allows them to respect the freedom and independence of Aries, who do the same in return. Aquarians can also flourish with Taureans, if the latter set aside their possessiveness. With Geminians, however, love is founded on the absence of constraints and on constant dialogue. Cancerians allow Aquarians to create and invent by managing all aspects of daily life. Aquarians admire Leos, but their union can only last if the former take an interest in what their partners are doing. Virgos find it difficult to bear an Aquarian partner's frivolity. With Librans, their compatibility is evident in both ideas and love. Aquarians attract Scorpios, who are drawn to their partners' mysterious genius, and they garner the respect of Sagittarians. Their spontaneity and enthusiasm turn the life of Capricorns upside down. Two Aquarians together, however, form an original couple because they care little for convention and live out their passions. Finally, between Pisceans and Aquarians there is a story of tenderness, mutual understanding and strong friendship.

JANVIER
Serie 360 Nr. 1

PASSIONATELY ORIGINAL

Aquarius

Aquarians are interested in a great many fields, but they give preference to originality. It is not always easy to understand their projects, as they are the only ones to have any control over them. They reject routine and prefer occupations that preserve their independence. Whatever their activities, they always manage to bring something new, and they can only bear their superiors if they give encouragement. They do not choose their occupation for money, but according to their passion. Aquarians are interested in computer science, robotics, physics, astronomy, aeronautics and all fields that contribute to progress and help improve the daily lives of humanity. Because they are altruistic, they come to the aid of the most destitute and idealize human values. Their professional relationships are amicable and are based on dialogue and the exchange of ideas, cooperation and solidarity. They can therefore be found in humanitarian organizations or associations that defend human rights. They also prefer the activities ruled by Uranus that are linked to the fields of communication and information, such as the press, television, radio, multimedia communications and social media. And finally, they like anything to do with science fiction.

JANVIER.
FÉVRIER.
XI
XII
LE VERSEAU.
LES POISSONS.
VÉRITABLE
EXTRAIT
DE VIANDE LIEBIG.
Le soleil entre dans ce signe vers le
21 Janvier.
Fable: Jupiter, sous la forme d'un aigle, enleva Ganymède, jeune prince d'une grande beauté, et le transporta au ciel pour remplacer Hébé comme échanson des dieux.
Les signes
du Zodiaque.
Le soleil entre dans ce signe vers le
18 Février.
Fable: Amphitrite rejoignit son époux Neptune dans un char traîné par deux dauphins.

PROMETHEUS

Aquarius

Prometheus was a Titan. His name means 'forward-thinker'. He was very intelligent and cunning, and many ancient Greek authors credit him with the creation of humanity. He was indeed said to have been tasked by Zeus to create mankind. His creatures were sturdy and stood on two legs. And to help them to survive, Prometheus gave them the sacred fire, which he had stolen from Olympus. He also taught them many techniques, such as metallurgy. However, his actions enraged Zeus, who decided to punish him by chaining him forever to a rock. An eagle came to him every day to devour his liver, which then grew back. Like this Titan, Aquarians have a dislike for convention and decorum. They are revolutionaries who need independence. In the myth, Prometheus embodies the visionary hero who helps humans by giving them fire, allowing them to create, innovate and improve their living conditions. This aim is shared by Aquarians, who by their fellowship, friendship and solidarity, do not hesitate to brave hardship in order to enable humanity to advance. They are willing to pay a high price to enable individuals to overcome restrictions and win their freedom.

PROMÉTHÉE. - 2. *Prométhée forme l'homme et Minerve lui donne le souffle.*

MOZART, A VISIONARY REBEL

Aquarius

Wolfgang Amadeus Mozart was born in Salzburg on 27 January 1756 and died in Vienna on 5 December 1791. His work was prolific despite his premature death at the age of thirty-five. He is considered the greatest composer of European classical music. His operas and music are performed all over the world. This piano and violin virtuoso was a veritable creative genius. A child prodigy, he began to give his first concerts at the age of five and wrote his first opera at the age of eleven. The moon in the house ruling the family implies that he had inherited his talents. In fact, his father was a musician. His sun sign, Aquarius, and the power of Uranus in his birth chart may partly explain his rebellious nature and his desire to emancipate himself from patrons who did not allow him creative freedom. He was a visionary and had some amazing insights. The sun conjunct Saturn aspect also made him a tireless and rigorous worker. His Virgo rising sign evidences his constant quest for perfection. In 1791, he composed two major masterpieces, *The Magic Flute* and *Requiem*, portentous signs of his Aquarian visionary quality.

108. MOZART

PISCES, GOOD SAMARITANS

Winter sign

Pisces, the constellation of the fish, is the sign of people born between 19 February and 20 March. Pisces has water as its element and is ruled by the planet Neptune. Its lucky day is Thursday and its lucky number is two. It has aquamarine as its stone, sky blue as its colour and manganese as its metal. Hyacinths are the favourite flowers of this sign. Its symbol depicts two fish swimming in opposite directions, signifying the dual nature of this sign. Pisceans are generous and infinitely compassionate. They are sensitive to human distress and devote themselves to humanitarian causes, revealing their sense of sacrifice and devotion. They use their resourcefulness to draw sympathy for their benefit. Pisceans are sensitive to the arts, especially music, and are very creative. They have a very intense emotional world and highly developed intuition. Their sixth sense guides them through any situation. They are easily influenced and hyperemotional, and they go where life takes them. They also know how to keep their secrets without ever revealing them. They are endowed with a vivid imagination and have a love for poetry and literature. Their inner lives are rich and full of dreams. There are two types of Pisceans. The first, known as Jupiterians, are materialistic and opportunistic. However, they are also empathetic and committed to defending the oppressed. The second, Neptunians, seek isolation and meditation, often turning to religion, asceticism and self-denial.

FÉVRIER
LES POISSONS
Le Bal masqué

MERGING INTO ONE

Pisces

Sensitive, receptive, permeable and idealistic Pisceans often allow themselves to be overwhelmed by their emotions. They seek an unusual, fusional and redeeming form of love that engages their compassion. Their sensitivity and intuition enable them to guide Aries to achieve their goals. They find Taureans reassuring because of their protective nature and sensuality. Pisceans want to merge with Geminians, who are afraid to commit and form attachments. Cancerians make them tender, affectionate and fanciful. Pisceans show Leos the admiration they deserve, and offer them their appreciation and support. They turn Virgos into dreamers. When Virgos come into contact with Pisceans, they lose their sense of reality and pragmatism and become more whimsical. Librans are the ideal match for Pisceans. With Scorpios, Pisceans find a partner with whom they can merge. Because they are both idealistic and generous, Pisceans and Sagittarians share their enthusiasm for others and travelling. Capricorns give them confidence in themselves by making them feel protected. When paired with Aquarians, Pisceans have their heads in the stars and this contact makes them more independent. When fully merged, two Pisceans together are uplifted. They have no need to communicate because they understand each other intuitively.

CHICORÉE NOUVELLE
CASIEZ & BOURGEOIS
à CAMBRAI
LES POISSONS

INSPIRED CAREGIVERS

Pisces

Because they are drawn to others, Pisceans tend to choose occupations in the social, medical and humanitarian fields. They genuinely like to assist, save and heal, which explains their involvement in major causes. They are attentive and always ready to be of service. In the hospital setting, they can be found as doctors, nurses, laboratory assistants and healthcare assistants. They can also be found in prison administration jobs. They have a close connection with the sea and love to sail and explore. They are also interested in shipping, shipbuilding, fishing and fish-farming. In medical astrology, this sign of Pisces corresponds to the feet. Consequently, Pisceans can be found making shoes and boots, and as chiropodists and podiatrists. Their creative side also draws them to the artistic professions. And because they are mystical, inspired and intuitive, they have an intense interest in the occult sciences. Indeed, seers, mediums, astrologers and mesmerists are often Pisceans. Pisceans are excellent when it comes to organizational design. They are also perfectly suited to teamwork. They are highly versatile and tend to change the direction of their careers several times. Their medium-like intuition and discernment make up for their lack of practicality, allowing them to succeed where least expected.

FÉVRIER
Les Giboulées.
HUNTLEY & PALMERS
BISCUITS
Reading & London
Les Poissons

PROTEUS
Pisces

In Greek mythology, Proteus is the son of Poseidon and personification of the unconscious that manifests itself in the form of dreams and inspiration. Homer referred to him in the *Odyssey* as the 'Old Man of the Sea' and as the herdsman of his father's seals. Because he was renowned for his gift of prophecy, sailors came to consult him. However, before they could know their destiny, they had to surprise him as he slumbered during the day with his seals in a cave away from the heat. Proteus took mischievous pleasure in shifting his shape into that of an animal, water or tree to escape. Nevertheless, his advice was always very sound. One day, a sea nymph advised a visitor to bind him and hold him to the ground as he slept in order to obtain a prophecy when he woke up. This myth is a good analogy for the sign of Pisces, as Pisceans have formidable intuition and a vivid imagination. Like Proteus, they find it difficult to express how they feel and prefer to run away rather than face a problem. They are also as elusive as Proteus. Pisceans immerse themselves in their environment, feel their surroundings and realize their emotional and spiritual nature by feeling they are entrusted with a mission.

Pag. 36.

UNE SIRÈNE PROTÉE TRITON

VICTOR HUGO, A PISCEAN WITH A FIGHTING SPIRIT

Pisces

Victor Hugo was born on 26 February 1802 in Besançon and died on 22 May 1885 in Paris. He was a humanist and one of the greatest writers and poets of his time. He was also a great politician. His desire as a teenager was 'to be Chateaubriand or nothing'. This sentence evidences his thirst for glory and recognition, which is expressed in his birth chart by the presence of Jupiter in Leo. His personality was enlivened by many contradictions. Saturn in Virgo indicates that he longed for peace and quiet, although he led a hectic worldly life. With the three planets of Venus, Pluto and Mercury, as well as the sun, in Pisces, Victor Hugo was the embodiment of his sign. He was intuitive, visionary and mysterious, and he had exceptional and receptive intelligence. He was often carried away by his emotions, which he reproduced in his visionary and almost medium-like writing through the creation of colourful characters. Venus in Pisces meant that he could never choose between his wife and his mistress Juliette Drouet. Mars in Aquarius, which has a strong presence in his birth chart, brought him enthusiasm and a generous fighting spirit. He was a passionate man, although he was sometimes misunderstood. And he had an incredible ability to bounce back from every ordeal he experienced in his life, just like the characters in his novels. He could also be both scathing and highly empathetic at the same time.

VICTOR HUGO
RUY BLAS
Victor Hugo

FURTHER READING

Barbault, André, *Astrologie : symboliques, calculs, interprétations*, Seuil, 2005.

Barbault, André, *L'Astrologie certifiée, Connaissances, Statistiques & Prévisions*, Seuil 2006.

Chermet-Carroy, Sylvie, *L'Astrologie médicale*, Trédaniel, mars 1988.

Chermet-Carroy, Sylvie, *Manuel pratique d'astrologie*, Trédaniel, 1996.

Giani, Patrick, *Les Trois Dimensions de votre thème astral*, Éditions du Rocher, 29 avril 2004.

Gorse, Julie, *Décrypter votre thème astral*, Hachette, 2019.

Legrand, Roland, *Cours complet d'astrologie pratique* : ABLAS (Français), 1er décembre 2017.

Orion, Rae, *L'Astrologie Poche Pour les Nuls*, First éditions, 5 janvier 2005.

Rudhyar, Dane, *Les Aspects astrologiques*, Éditions du Rocher, 1997.

Rudhyar, Dane, *L'Astrologie de la personnalité*, Librairie de Médicis, 2002.

Tanti, Fabienne, *Les Douze Signes du zodiaque*, Aedis, 2015.

ALSO AVAILABLE

THE LITTLE BOOK OF BIRDS	9782812316364
THE LITTLE BOOK OF CATS	9782812317408
THE LITTLE BOOK OF DOGS	9782812318580
THE LITTLE BOOK OF ESOTERICA	9782379641343
THE LITTLE BOOK OF MEDICINAL PLANTS	9782812319815
THE LITTLE BOOK OF NEW YORK	9782812315329
THE LITTLE BOOK OF PARIS	9782812313318
THE LITTLE BOOK OF ROSES	9782379640810
THE LITTLE BOOK OF THE LANGUAGE OF FLOWERS	9782812318924
THE LITTLE BOOK OF THE MOON	9782379641046
THE LITTLE BOOK OF TREES	9782379641039
THE LITTLE BOOK OF VERSAILLES	9782812317804
THE LITTLE BOOK OF WITCHES	9782379641053

ABOUT US

E/P/A publishes high-quality coffee table and reference books.

Combining a highly visual approach with well-researched content and the highest standards of production, E/P/A offers books on Music, Film, Transport, Nature, Adventure, Science, History, and Hobbies.

E/P/A also publishes gift books under its Papier Cadeau imprint.

E/P/A is part of the Hachette Livre Group.

All images are from the private collection of Éditions Papier Cadeau, except page 17 © Print Collector/Getty France; page 21 © Hulton Archive/Getty France; page 39 © CCI/Bridgeman Images; page 43 © Lee/Leemage; page 45 © Hulton Archive/Getty France; page 79 © Bob Thomas/Popperfoto/Getty France; page 89 © Popperfoto/Getty France; page 127 © MEPL/Bridgeman Images; page 167 © Florilegius/Leemage.
Cover: Flat 1 © Picturenow/Getty France and background © Éditions Papier Cadeau.

For the original edition:

www.papier-cadeau.fr

For the current edition:

Editorial director: Jérôme Layrolles
Editorial Manager: Laurence Lehoux
Coordinating editor: Franck Friès
Proofreading: Mireille Touret
Art director: Charles Ameline
Production: Cécile Alexandre-Tabouy
Layout and Photogravure: CGI

Direct sales and partnerships:
partenariats-epa@hachette-livre.fr
Press Relations: epa@hachette-livre.fr

English translation and proofreading by John Ripoll and Ruby Morris for Cillero & de Motta

Published by Papier Cadeau
(58, rue Jean-Bleuzen 92170 Vanves Cedex)
Printed in February 2021
ISBN 978-2-37964-133-6
3230057